Compassion @work

David Baumgartner
Sam Bresler
Madiha Chughtai
Heather Dilmagani
Laurie Copperman-Friedman
Angela Hurd Greer
Lyle S. Hanna
Paula H. Harvey
Michelle Hollingshead
Dr. Milli McIntosh
Tonia Morris
Stacey Oliver-Knappe
Jason Sackett
Dr. Amy M. Smith
Ben St. Clair
Carole Stizza
Shelly Trent
Laura Hillerich Wood

Creating Workplaces That Engage the Human Spirit

A Collection of Insights from Leading HR and OD Experts

Compassion@Work
Creating Workplaces That Engage the Human Spirit

Published by Silver Tree Publishing, a division of Silver Tree Communications, LLC (Kenosha, WI).
www.SilverTreeCommunications.com

Contributing Authors:

David R. Baumgartner	Dr. Milli McIntosh
Sam Bresler	Tonia Morris
Madiha Chughtai	Stacey Oliver-Knappe
Heather Dilmagani	Jason Sackett
Laurie Copperman-Friedman	Dr. Amy M. Smith
Angela Hurd Greer	Ben St. Clair
Lyle S. Hanna	Carole Stizza
Paula H. Harvey	Shelly Trent
Michelle Hollingshead	Laura Hillerich Wood

Editing by:
Barb Cahoon Wang
Kate Colbert

Cover design and typesetting by:
Courtney Hudson

First edition, November 2017

Compassion@Work is the first volume in the @Work Series from Silver Tree Publishing, in collaboration with Cathy Fyock, LLC.

ISBN: 978-0-9991491-5-7

Library of Congress Control Number: 2017959051

Created in the United States of America

Acknowledgements
from the Publishers

We want to express our gratitude to the authors who have contributed to this anthology. We value the faith that each author had in us. With highly personal stories and insights about leaders and organizations who put compassion at the heart of the workplace, our 18 amazing authors generously gave us the pleasure of working with them to compile this anthology. We treasure these stories even more because, throughout the authoring and publishing process, we had the chance to get to know each author as an individual. Their powerful stories, keen insights and important practical advice were universally shared with enthusiasm, professionalism and most important, compassion. It has been a privilege to work with them all.

We also would like to extend our gratitude to Sharon Armstrong of the SAA Trainers and Consultants Network, a free referral service for HR, OD, trainers, coaches and keynote speakers. Sharon is an HR consultant and author who was very helpful to us as we set out to develop this anthology. She can be reached at 202-333-0644 or online at www.trainersandconsultants.net.

With the underlying theme of compassion, this anthology demonstrates the breadth of the ways that compassion can be expressed in the workplace, from individual acts to formal processes, as well as the deep and lasting impact that compassion can have not only on the recipient but on the individual, team and organization that acts with compassion. By sharing their stories, these authors show practical and accessible ways that human resource leaders, chief executives and other professionals can employ, teach and support the value of placing compassion at the heart of the workplace. We are proud to share their experiences and important insights with you. Enjoy.

— Kate Colbert and Cathy Fyock

Table of Contents

♥

Chapter 1

♥

David R. Baumgartner
SHRM-SCP, SPHR, SSGB, CNA

"Compassion@Work – Who Cares?"

Compassion, like any other value, is in the eyes of the beholder. Values have different meaning to different people in different roles. Are values personal barometers for my personal life or the way I want to lead my team at work? Are values driven and applied differently across different small teams within a larger organization, or are the values established at the top ultimately used to set the tone for the expected behavior from many employees across a broad geographic area?

No two people perceive values the same way. How one person perceives compassion, respect, responsiveness or any other value will be different from the next. To reduce conflict that comes from perception differences, organizations, work groups, teams and families can reduce conflict by identifying values that govern expected behavior and create an understanding of behaviors that complement and or conflict with the values. In this chapter, I'll share my journey of learning to articulate, identify and hardwire expectations around service values, including the exercise of compassion at work.

Birth of the Four Rules

The first practical application of values started at home, when our oldest daughter Lauren was about 14 years old, and she was playing me and her mother against each other. We were having one of those discussions when I let her know that I had to have a relationship with her until she was 18; after that, it was as much my decision as hers. As the conversation continued, I suggested that the way our relationship would evolve during the next four years was up to her. Continuing, I said, "I'm not a fan of purple hair or earrings in places other than ears, but I'll deal with that if we can comply with the Four Rules: Trust, Respect, Balance and Grades."

We talked about decision-making and illustrating a timeline, and we talked about having a long view. The whole discussion lasted 15 minutes.

Little did anyone know that the Four Rules would become the foundation for teaching Lauren and our three other children how to think about their decisions. Whenever one of the kids was making a decision that I took issue with, we'd talk about it; then I'd ask, "which of the Four Rules does this conflict with?" We would chat. At the end of the discussion, the final questions were, "Are mistakes good or bad?" They would respond, "Good!" My response was, "When?" They would quickly answer, "When you learn from them!"

This became our ritual whenever one of the kids made decisions we wanted to talk about:

1. Clarify what happened using questions, not accusatory statements.

2. Clarify how the issue conflicted with our core values: the Four Rules.

3. Conclude with shaking it off, and moving forward with the commitment that we have learned from the process.

Today, Lauren is more than 30 years old and we have three grandchildren. The Four Rules became so ingrained that, on occasion, I've even received a text from one of the kids saying that they had told a friend about the Four Rules and the timeline.

Signature Healthcare and the Sacred Six

Fast forward 12 years; Signature Healthcare CEO/President Joe Steier commissioned a service value study sent to 18,000 employees to identify the values that make a great care-giver. From that study, the Sacred Six was introduced: Compassion, Teamwork, Respect, Integrity, Patience and Positivity.

At the time, I was serving as an HR consultant for Signature and had recently been assigned the task of onboarding a newly acquired region in Indiana. A few months after the acquisition, Signature conducted its routine nine-month employee engagement survey; the Indiana region came in last place out of 11 regions. Fortunately, the newly promoted regional vice president, Kimberly Vermilyea, knew that the way you achieve results is through employees. She understood that the further you get away from the customer, the less control you have over the customer experience. Like the Four Rules, we used the Sacred Six as a critical component for onboarding that region to adopt the Signature culture.

As a region, we took every opportunity to discuss the Sacred Six and gave examples of behaviors to look for. We set an expectation that leaders would learn to recognize employee actions that support Sacred Six values, and we would hold each other accountable for behaviors that conflicted with these values.

Seeing a Value in Action

Being able to see a behavior and then connect it to a value is not as intuitive as one would think. It took time for leadership to be able to see and understand how to connect an employee action into one or more of the Sacred Six, especially when the performance issue was not tangible. Routinely, a local CEO would call, asking how to handle a member of their leadership team who was meeting the technical aspects of their job, yet something was missing. They would use vague terms, such as the employee is "lazy," has a "poor attitude," or is not a "team-player."

Just like the conversations with my kids, I'd start asking questions: "Why do you say that?" "Can you give me specific examples of things this individual does that would make you say they are lazy or has a poor attitude or is not a team-player?"

After a few minutes of letting them talk and ask questions, I'd say, "That is perfect information. Can you tell me which Sacred Six values those behaviors conflict with?" You could almost feel the relief come through the phone as they connected the definition of a value to the ability to see the value in action.

Hardwiring Values at a Divisional Level: See It in Each Other

Nine months later, during the next employee engagement cycle, the Indiana region went from last to 4th place out of 11 regions. The results caught the eye of the divisional leader, Mark Worrley, who asked me to assume responsibility for coordinating efforts with regional operational leaders to elevate the employee and customer experience.

Being yet another layer further from the customer, the challenge to embed values became more difficult because of two major factors:

1. At the division level, we had to work through regional leadership who had operational challenges; any cultural solution had to be simple and recognizable.

2. We noticed when a "rock star" CEO at the local level would leave, it wasn't uncommon to have cultural setback — leading to more operational challenges — because the culture was built around the CEO's personality and specific training.

To solve the problems, we introduced a simple research-based process: See it in Each Other. First, research came from our consummate teacher, CEO/President Joe Steier. Steier introduced senior leadership to an *American Behavior Scientist* study (Losada & Heaphy, 2004, p. 8) that identified ways to maintain high-performance teams. One of three specific things leaders can do to support high performance is to provide positive reinforcements significantly more often than they provide negative corrections (ideally at a ratio of 5.6 positive reinforcements for each one negative correction). The next study was a Cornell study (Hinklin & Schreisheim, 2004, p. 369) suggesting that positive reinforcement increases role clarity, effectiveness and satisfaction.

The concept of See it in Each Other is simple:

1. We kept reminding local leadership that, although their daily lives are filled with operational whirlwinds, many employees around them are doing little things that sustain quality service, exceptional customer experience and good team work.

2. We asked local leadership to spend three minutes during their morning daily huddle discussing things they saw that they'd like to see more of.

3. Then, throughout the next few days as members of the leadership team saw the employee, they would let them know that the

leadership team was talking about them; and they would thank them for their efforts.

These leaders were encouraged to keep it simple; they didn't need to recognize 10 or 15 people per day. If they would consistently recognize four to six people per day on different shifts, in different departments, then over the course of the month, the culture of recognition would take root and blossom.

This process helped overcome the two challenges identified above. First, the process was simple to explain, avoided complicated forms and tracking processes; and when a member of the regional leadership team attended a morning huddle, they would be able to observe whether they spent a few moments practicing the See it in Each Other technique. Next, as middle managers began to understand the power of recognition, they didn't need a "rock star" CEO to drive the culture. It provided more stability through top local leadership change.

Keep It Genuine and Avoid Vagueness

We didn't expect every member of the leadership team to provide a recognition every day; one or two per week was plenty. During a follow-up visit to see how one location was adopting See it in Each Other, I attended the morning huddle. When they were ready to wrap up, I asked, "Didn't have any recognition today?" One member of the leadership team said, "I'm not going to fake it."

We talked as a team to understand what she meant; at the conclusion, the team realized there is a difference between their styles and being genuine. They perceived that we were asking them to be extroverted and bubbly when that is not who they are. They were encouraged to be themselves, and to use their own words to have a genuine conversation with the employee. They didn't need to offer a dissertation — just a simple thank you for the way the employee compassionately handled a customer during a difficult time, or the specific way the individual jumped in to help a peer.

Avoiding vagueness is the key to getting the specific desired behaviors. Telling someone they displayed great teamwork doesn't tell the employee what you like. Saying, "We had good team work today because everyone jumped in when we had the late admission. Although this was not Susan's patient, she started the paperwork, allowing Jill to greet the patient and begin the assessment." This is a 15- to 20-second conversation, and now Susan and Jill both know exactly what teamwork looks like.

The Power of Recognition

Don't underestimate the power of recognition. Research at Baylor University (Tsang, 2006, p. 139) suggests that people who are grateful are more likely to act in a pro-social manner, with gratitude being defined as an emotional response toward other people and not to oneself. The research also suggests that people who are grateful are less likely to engage in destructive interpersonal behavior.

What does that mean to leaders? No matter what the demands we have on our schedules, take time every day to look around to see employees doing the little things you want to see more of; then tell them "thank you." It's great to get a recognition on the bulletin board, but this can't match the genuine compliment from a supervisor or a peer.

♥ *Try it today. Say "thank you" to a person for something specific, and watch the expression on their face. Then, see if you don't get more of the same behavior in the future.*

Getting Results and Keeping Them

By no means is this a magic bullet; recognition and reinforcement of service values are one part of our divisional/organizational intention to achieve consistent customer and employee experience across different regions through different leaders with different personalities. However, where local CEOs adopted the process of recognition and reinforcement of values, along with a couple other simple processes, they could see a change in their employee culture in a matter of weeks. One facility saw such a dramatic reduction in the number of customer complaints, it affected the reputation in the community within a year. At the divisional level, on a CEO survey, our team went from last place of three divisions to first place in one year because we simplified and clarified divisional goals and expectations on a range of topics, including customer and employee experience.

The challenge is creating a sense of urgency for consistency. The process was so simple and took so little time each day that it was easy to forget, or to let it go "just for today" because of other priorities. If values are important, then invest time "all the time" to recognize and reinforce behavior that supports these values.

Finding the Balance

Organizations that want a consistent culture need to find the balance between teaching principles and establishing visible processes. Most people know that Chick-fil-A is a faith-based organization, yet do they build their customer experience by telling employees to practice the Golden Rule? No way! They implement a simple stimulus/response process. When the employee hears "thank you" from a customer, they respond with, "It is my pleasure."

Chick-fil-A has training intended to build leadership knowledge around concepts that are important to them. They also build simple processes that are recognizable regardless of the location or the local leader.

So, Who Cares?

I started this piece by asking, "Compassion@Work. Who cares?" Then I have spent the whole chapter discussing anything but compassion; instead, I addressed structures that support organizational values — including compassion. As the deadline approached to complete this chapter, I found myself flying to Florida two days before Hurricane Irma made landfall to work with Signature HealthCare facilities' evacuation, and then deal with the aftermath of this Category 4 storm. Compassion — one of Signature's Sacred Six values — was evident in the way employees worked with customers around the clock during that very difficult and stressful time.

Was it lucky that the employees showed compassion, or was it the fact that one of Signature's Sacred Six values is compassion? My opinion is that it takes both!

Why embed values, including compassion? At home, we want our children to learn to make decisions based on sound reasoning and critical thinking. The Four Rules gave our family common language to discuss decision-making. Signature introduced the Sacred Six after they had grown to 18,000 employees in approximately 120 locations, with new leaders continually joining the company. During this time of rapid growth, Joe Steier didn't want to lose the values that made Signature a special place to work.

In 2004, I started working with Consolo Services Group when they had two employees. Today, it has almost 100 employees around the country, and most of that growth occurred in the past couple of years. Like

Signature, when Consolo was small, the organization had a family feel, and it was easy to stay connected. As they grew, President Greg Kite couldn't stay as connected to all the employees as he wished. He knew he had to do something to maintain the employee commitment that had enabled the company to grow. In 2016, Consolo rolled out their service values with an expectation that leaders look for and recognize behaviors that support their values. Recently, an employee said, "I'm grateful to work for such an amazing company with an outstanding boss!"

Families, large companies and small startups can all benefit from identifying values that are important to their culture, and by being intentional in embedding them. Compassion: I would hope everyone wants it at work. The question is, "What are leaders going to do to define it and maintain it?"

References

Losada, M., & Heaphy, E. (2004). The role of positivity and connectivity in the performance of business teams. *American Behavioral Scientist*, 47, 740-765. http://dx.doi.org/10.1177/0002764203260208

Hinklin, T. R., & Schreisheim, C. A. (2004, November 10, 2004). If you don't hear from me, you are doing fine; the effects of management nonresponse to employee performance. *Cornell Hotel and Restaurant Administration Quarterly*, 45, 362-372. http://dx.doi.org/10.1177/0010880404270061

Tsang, J. (2006). Gratitude and prosocial behavior: an experimental test of gratitude. *Psychology Press*, 20, 138-148. http://dx.doi.org/10.1080/02699930500172341

About the Author

David R. Baumgartner, SHRM-SCP,
SPHR, SSGB, CNA

With more than 20 years of senior-level HR
experience, David has worked with operators
to achieve organizational metrics through
clearly defined objectives and effective
messaging that creates a collaborative focus.

David's experience includes working on
mergers and acquisitions; home office, divisional and regional roles; and risk manage-
ment. In all projects, the goal is to align organizational goals to create
cultures of highly-engaged customer-focused employees. Because David
is dedicated to the role that customer feedback plays in overall organizational health, he also carries net promoter score (NPS) certification.

His accomplishments include improving engagement in an acquired
region from worst to top-tier performer, improving divisional leadership
scores from worst to first, and improving organizational team focus.

David's current assignment is VP of Spirituality for Signature Healthcare,
where he is part of the team that guides the chaplain team and spirituality for Signature's 120-plus facilities. In addition to his work at
Signature, David partners with his wife, Karen to provide HR consulting
services to a small number of organizations through their company HR
Partnership, LLC. In his free time, David enjoys spending time with his
wife, children and grandchildren — grillin' and chillin', boating, in the
mountains, biking or golfing with his son-in-law.

Learn more and contact David:
DBaumgartner@Tresane.com
Twitter.com/drbaumgartner
LinkedIn.com/in/drbaumgartnerky

Chapter 2

♥

Sam Bresler, Madiha Chughtai and Heather Dilmagani

"Compassion@Work – Saying Goodbye with Compassion"

In the spring of 2017, Brandman University was required to plan and execute a reduction-in-force process affecting approximately two dozen valued employees. Saying goodbye to these employees was a difficult, personally challenging experience, yet absolutely necessary to ensure our university's continued ability to deliver its award-winning programs to our engaged adult learners. This is our story of how we infused compassion, as well as thoughtful consideration, into this reduction-in-force process.

Background

Brandman University is a private, non-profit university with 12,000 students, and is a member of the Chapman University System. Chapman University, founded in 1861, is one of the oldest, private non-profit universities in California. Chapman University College was one of Chapman University's eight colleges, offering high-quality programs to adult learners. On June 1, 2008, Chapman and Chapman University College became separate universities; and in February 2009, the Western Association of Schools and Colleges (WASC) formally recognized University College of Chapman University (UCCU) as a separately accredited institution within the newly established Chapman University System; it remained dedicated to extending the Chapman education to working adult students online and through a network of 26 campuses in California and Washington.

As the result of a major gift in January 2009 by Joyce Brandman and the Brandman Foundation — strong advocates of education for working adults — the Board of Regents voted to change the name of the newly created institution from UCCU to Brandman University.

Higher and Adult Education: Market Challenges

Higher education organizations have faced increasing business challenges in recent years. These include greater institutional accountability for student outcomes and the demand to create capabilities among graduates that have more immediate workplace relevance. Institutions of higher education also must contend with flat enrollment growth, changing demographics and an increased competitive environment that continues to limit institutional tuition increases. The industry overall faces greater competition from two sources: new organizations that provide alternative channels for higher education, and an increasing number of traditional universities now delivering online educational programs. Technology is offering unprecedented avenues to transform the higher education experience, including adaptive learning and virtual teaching assistants.

Impact of Current Market Challenges on Brandman University

Brandman University — despite its plethora of award-winning, market-focused programs geared to the needs of the engaged, adult learner — has not been immune to the market challenges that higher education faces. Enrollment growth, which had been consistent, began to diminish in recent years and the university encountered actual enrollment declines during the 2015-2016 and 2016-2017 academic years.

Despite efforts to reduce discretionary expenditures throughout the University, it became clear that a more significant initiative was required to align expenses with enrollment-driven revenues. As a result, the senior executive leadership team concluded that a reduction in force was necessary, and turned to the Human Resources team to plan and execute that process in a very short timeframe. The planning and execution needed to be completed in several weeks.

Planning

♥ *When the Human Resources team was given the challenge of planning the reduction in force process, we wanted to ensure that our approach was both operationally efficient and preserved the dignity and respect of each of the affected employees during and following the transition. It mattered to us that we find a way to say goodbye with compassion.*

Layoff planning began by creating selection criteria to guide our line managers and leaders through the process of determining the positions to select for elimination, and then ultimately identify the employees who would be directly impacted. A large part of this phase was working with line managers and leaders to ensure that the layoffs were not a means for them to terminate an employee for deficient performance or simply as an opportunity to be able to move them out of the organization. This was one of the more difficult phases of the layoff process; many line managers and leaders could not understand why they could not select their lowest-performing team member for layoff.

To help leaders understand how to select the appropriate position to eliminate, we explained that when a position is eliminated, the outcome needs to reflect exactly that construct: the elimination of a "position" that is no longer needed. Therefore, if a poor performer is in a job that is no longer needed, we have a desired outcome. However, if the poor performer is in a job that is needed, and the leader intends to eliminate that individual's employment (and then refill that position), we are not acting in accordance with the intent of an ethical, legally justifiable reduction in force process. Doing so can create distrust among the affected employees, as well as among those who remain in the organization.

It was vital to ensure that the justification and selection of eliminated positions was based on a collective understanding that the positions selected were those that were least needed within the University. After we developed a list of positions to be eliminated, in consultation with legal counsel, we reviewed the affected individuals to ensure their selection did not result in a discriminatory impact.

The next phase of the layoff process was deciding what separation support would be provided. Brandman's reduction in force policy provides severance pay in an amount correlated to years of service with the institution. It was recently revised to provide that even employees with less than one year of service receive at least two weeks of severance pay. In addition to providing severance pay, we believed it was both appropriate and necessary to allow these employees the opportunity to receive resources that would assist them in looking forward to the next phase of their careers, therefore easing the challenges of their transition. We achieved this objective by planning to offer career transition/outplacement services for a period of three months; this included individual career coaching, seminars, workshops and access to a specialized job search network and website.

The final step of the planning process was to prepare our line managers for the critical roles they would play in the reduction-in-force process. The HR team created a reduction-in-force process guidance document for leaders, which included pre-meeting preparation tasks, behavioral tips for the reduction-in-force meeting focused on how to treat the employee, and topics to avoid during the reduction-in-force conversation. We also created a list of issues that could go wrong in the meeting and guidance for how to deal with any emotional reactions. Finally, we provided specific guidance on follow-up steps in communicating with employees who were not directly impacted by the reduction-in-force process. Our team created scripts for the reduction-in-force meetings to share with each leader participating in lay-off conversations. The intention was to create a seamless communications process that demonstrated the partnership of line management and the HR team.

Execution

As reduction-in-force conversations took place, the goal of the HR team was to ensure that the affected employees not only understood the information being presented to them, but were empowered to take the necessary transition-related steps with clarity and confidence. Individual and customized packets were given to each affected employee; these included personalized documents, such as relevant benefit information, severance payment documents, information on unemployment and contact information for HR team members who could assist with any questions.

Layoffs are stressful and often not expected by the employee; therefore, it was essential to provide the affected employees with all relevant information in print to review and absorb after they had overcome the initial shock of notification. By ensuring that the benefit information they were receiving was not generic, but was instead customized to the specific benefits each individual was enrolled in, the affected employees were given concrete evidence that the institution valued their contributions; the University and our HR team took the time to provide materials that were tailored expressly to individual needs and avoided inundating these employees with unnecessary information.

We had earlier decided that the reduction-in-force decision should be directly communicated by each employee's supervisor. Our rationale was to enable the employee to hear the news from a familiar face and to allow the genuine compassion of these leaders to be evident in these discussions. In addition, we recognized that the HR team at Brandman is centrally located; some of the layoffs occurred at our campuses located in multiple states. It would not send a compassionate message to deliver the reduction-in-force decision remotely, and communicated by a person these employees have never met.

Leaders were asked to send meeting notifications to their affected direct reports. All meetings took place in rooms that were located next to each other. Each room was staffed with a HR practitioner, a box of tissues and the individual employee packets. In addition, on-site outplacement career coaches were available to speak to each affected individual immediately after they were notified of the layoff. For our remote campus locations, a career coach contacted each individual within 24 hours of the layoff conversation. The discussions with the career coaches allowed the affected employees to gain confidence by offering powerful tools as well as professional and peer resources to assist with a successful career transition process.

Our IT department was given a schedule to follow for system access removal; we wanted to ensure that access to systems was removed no earlier or later than when the layoff would occur. The last thing we wanted was for an individual to discover they were being laid off by being prematurely locked out of the system. These details are very important in coordinating a reduction in force, and we believe these small details made a difference in the employee experience.

Outcomes, Impact and the Role of Compassion

Given the impact of the reduction in force on the affected employees, their leaders, the institution as a whole and the HR professionals who were actively involved, the outcome and impact of this process should be examined from multiple perspectives.

First, the process required an exchange to take place between the institution and every affected employee. Each offer of severance pay, as well as individualized career transition support, was conditioned on the employee signing and returning (in a specific timeframe) a tailored separation agreement. The operational focus of the exchange was straightforward: the University offered substantial financial and career transition support — delivered with great care, clarity and compassion — in exchange for the employee agreeing to refrain from any legal action against the institution. We are happy to report that each of the affected employees signed and returned their separation agreements within the specified response timeframes.

In addition, we received subsequent communications from several of the affected employees thanking us for the approach that we used, and expressing gratitude for both the severance payments and the individualized career transition support. Many of these former employees continue to serve as ambassadors for the University, a factor that positively impacts our ability to attract and retain the talent needed to ensure the University's ongoing growth.

Compassion is defined in the *Merriam-Webster Dictionary* (online edition) as "sympathetic consciousness of others' distress, together with a desire to alleviate it." The individual layoff meetings were difficult for everyone involved, including the HR professionals. However, we strongly believe that we demonstrated a powerful sense of compassion through:

1. The design of the process
2. The preparation of the necessary materials
3. The organized way the notification process was executed, and
4. A continued and strong focus on alleviating any unnecessary concerns that those individuals might have had.

While the concept of being laid off may not be viewed as a compassionate act, HR professionals can and should choose to display thoughtful compassion throughout the process.

Afterword

In recent months, the University has begun to recover, and is now showing evidence of stronger enrollment growth. Contacts have continued between a number of the employees impacted by the reduction in force and their leaders, with a specific focus on future employment opportunities with the University. At the time of the creation of this chapter, the University has already taken steps to rehire the first of the affected employees, with opportunities for additional rehiring remaining as a possibility in future months.

We believe that the desire of those employees to return to the employ of Brandman University — coupled with leadership's desire to rehire them — represents an extraordinary outcome; it is an outcome that reflects favorably on the reputational capital of the University, and is one that could not have occurred without the thoughtful and compassionate manner in which the reduction-in-force process was conceptualized, planned and executed.

We additionally believe that HR professionals facing the need to plan and execute a reduction-in-force action should consider carefully the need for balance, addressing the needs of their respective organizations as well as the employees directly affected by the process. A compassionate mindset can be a powerful force in ensuring multiple positive outcomes.

About the Authors

Sam Bresler, PhD, SHRM-SCP, SPHR

Dr. Sam Bresler has more than 40 years of experience as a practitioner, leader and educator in Human Resource Management. Bresler currently serves as Special Assistant to the Provost and Professor of Human Resources and Business Administration at Brandman University, Irvine, CA, where he supports academic initiatives that create positive, transformational change among the University's adult student populations and the organizations they serve.

In 1998, Sam joined Chapman/Brandman University as a member of the Adjunct faculty, and in August 2011, he became a full-time faculty member of Brandman University's School of Business and Professional Studies (SBPS); he became its Associate Dean in August 2012. In October 2012, Sam assumed responsibility for leading the University's Human Resources, Learning and Development function as Assistant Vice Chancellor, and later, as its Associate Vice Chancellor.

Prior to joining Brandman, Sam served as Vice President for Human Resources for the western region of SAIC, a large, diversified technical services and solutions provider to U.S. federal agency clients, where he also led the Learning and Leadership Development function.

Bresler earned a PhD in Education from the University of Pennsylvania and an MBA in Management, with a specialization in Personnel Administration, from the University's Wharton Graduate Division. In 2015, he received SHRM-SCP Certification and, since 1996, has been working as a life-certified Senior Professional in Human Resources.

Long active in volunteer service to the HR profession, Sam served on the National Board of Directors for the Society for Human Resource Management Foundation from 1999-2004, and was President of the Foundation Board in 2002. Currently, he is a member of the SHRM Foundation's Leadership Circle, and continues to serve as a member of a National Item Writing Panel for the Human Resource Certification Institute's PHR and SPHR certification examinations. Sam loves international travel, and has visited every continent except Antarctica. He is devoted to reading at least two books each week and is most interested in history, political science, alternative history and science fiction.

Learn more and contact Sam:
samueljbresler@msn.com
Facebook.com/Samuel.J.Bresler
LinkedIn.com/in/SamBresler

Madiha Chughtai, PHR, SHRM-CP

Madiha Chughtai has more than 10 years of experience as a Human Resource professional, and has assumed roles of increasing responsibility in the field of Human Resources. Madiha joined Brandman University in 2012, and is currently the University's Director of Employee Relations and Title IX Coordinator.

Madiha earned her Bachelors in Psychology from the University of California Los Angeles in 2007, and a Master's of Science in Human Resources, with a specialization in Organizational Leadership, from Chapman University in 2010. She received her SHRM-SCP Certification in 2015.

Madiha is a California native, where she currently resides with her husband and young daughter. In their free time, Madiha and her husband love traveling and experiencing new cultures. Recently, they took their toddler to Thailand, where they snorkeled and fed elephants.

Learn more and contact Madiha:
chughtai@brandman.edu
LinkedIn.com/in/Madiha-Chughtai-PHR-SHRM-CP-088b849b/

Heather Dilmagani, PHR, SHRM-CP

Heather Dilmagani joined Brandman University in 2011, and has more than 10 years of Human Resources experience. In her career, she has worked to implement strategies pertaining to wellness, benefits, talent acquisition, performance, engagement and systems. She is currently the Director of Human Resources Operations at Brandman University, where she oversees various functional areas. Heather is committed to working with leaders throughout the organization to address issues and offer strategy solutions in the areas of compensation, benefits, talent acquisition, performance, systems and employee engagement.

Heather received a BA in Political Science from California State University, Long Beach, and earned a certification as a Professional in Human Resources (PHR) in 2013. She received her SHRM-CP certification in 2015. Heather is a Southern California native who enjoys spending time with her husband and son. They love cooking up new creations in the kitchen and attending baseball games at the Big A (Angel Stadium)!

Learn more and contact Heather:
heatherzadeh@gmail.com
LinkedIn.com/in/HeatherDilmagani

Chapter 3

♥

Laurie Copperman-Friedman

"It's Not Personal: Tools and Strategies for Being More Compassionate at Work, and Not Taking Things Personally"

It's not personal; yet many leaders find themselves taking their employees' behavior as personal. Consider, for instance, the employee who is constantly questioning your directives, who is always late with his or her report, or who says "yes" to you but does something else. What about someone who solicits your opinion, but never follows your advice?

How do you interpret this behavior? It may be natural to experience such employee behavior as personal. However, taking employee behavior personally is the least productive way to create a more compassionate work environment!

This chapter will highlight skills and tools to manage your emotional reactions, and to model improved communication and heightened compassion in the workplace. A high percentage of arguments are aggravated by tense emotions. Volatile emotions are counterproductive and should be avoided at every opportunity. When you practice skills and tools to avoid reacting personally, you are more likely to communicate and lead with compassion and support.

Compassion, as defined by Webster's dictionary, is sympathetic consciousness of others' distress together with a desire to alleviate it. Sounds like a quality most leaders would say they have, yet research suggests there is an epidemic of disengaged workers in our workforce. For your consideration, employee disengagement has less to do with one's job, and more with how employees are treated at work. As an executive coach and business consultant, I spend time guiding leaders to value their employees by leading with compassion and accountability. Learning to communicate without reacting emotionally is a fundamental leadership skill that is essential to building a highly engaged, compassionate workforce.

Overview: Why Do You Care?

Studies consistently find that an engaged workforce is a higher-performing workforce. Higher engagement is linked with higher profits; "most notably, higher employee engagement is linked to increased productivity (18%); higher customer satisfaction (12%); and lower voluntary turnover (51%)." ("Best Practices White Paper," http://lsaglobal. com/what-we-do/employee-engagement-survey/.)

The most recent U.S. results from the semi-annual Employment Engagement Index presented in the *Gallup Management Journal* indicates that "Only 29 percent of employees are actively engaged in their jobs. These employees work with passion and feel a profound connection to their companies. Moreover, 54 percent of employees are not engaged. These employees have essentially "checked out," sleepwalking through their workday and putting time — but not passion — into their work. In addition, it has been shown that 17 percent of employees are actively disengaged. These employees are busy acting out their unhappiness, undermining what their engaged co-workers are trying to accomplish."

("What Engages Employees the Most, or the Ten C's of Employee Engagement," http://iveybusinessjournal.com.)

Marshall Goldsmith, executive coach, thought-leader and author of *What Got You Here, Won't Get You There*, hypothesizes that the five most important words a leader can ask are: "How can I be better?"

This chapter will cover tools and strategies for "becoming a better leader" by improving communication, being more compassionate, and positively engaging the workforce. Topics will include:

- Thinking vs. feeling
- QTIP problem-solving
- Separating the person from the issue, and
- Leading with compassion — and accountability.

Thinking vs. Feeling

So, if we know employee engagement is linked to workforce success, why are so many employees disengaged? *Taking things personally!* When we take things personally, we weaken our engagement from our responsibilities. For example, have you ever thought an employee doesn't care when he/she does sloppy work? Even if it is true, what happens when your feelings get into the driver's seat? "What?" you say. "You don't care about my feelings?" Yes! "I care about you; I care about what you think, but I don't care about your feelings." (*The Sherpa Guide — Process-Driven Executive Coaching*, Brenda Corbett and Judith Coleman, pp. 1380139.) Your feelings are driven by an accumulation of your knowledge, past experiences, ego and values, and not facts. The reflective loop between our beliefs and the data we use to create meaning is frequently derailed by our emotions. For example, if you believe your opinions are not valued, you may automatically feel, "They don't value me," even in situations where the decision-making had nothing to do with you. An emotional response is often an automatic, unconscious response. Like smelling French fries and salivating! What is visible is your behavior.

How do you know if you are taking things personally? You react with your feelings before thinking. Some examples of emotional reactions include:

- Yelling
- Eye rolling
- Crying
- Stonewalling
- Emotional emails (those emails you wish you had not sent!)
- Shutting people down, through tone of voice or sharp words
- Anger, and
- Disengaging.

Can you think of additional emotional behaviors, either in yourself or others?

Our Blind Spot

STOP being guided by your emotions. A client recently told me that he had a direct report who was constantly complaining to fellow workers about him. He was not getting the job done and was a "problem child." I asked my client how he was supporting his employee's development? "I am not. I hate being around him." My response was, "It's not about you!" When you find yourself feeling frustrated and angry, thus taking things personally, STOP! It is time to redirect your energy to employee engagement and satisfaction.

Employee Engagement is Personal

The impact of employee engagement in the workforce is personal. Yet, when we take things personally we are not leading with compassion. For example, consider the employee who requires continuous reviews and rewrites to their reports. They get upset every time you suggest changes; they argue. Faced with someone who is upset, do you find that your negative emotions get into the driver's seat? If you react emotionally, your reactions become the obstacle to a successful communication. What is the cost if you get angry, and you get exasperated and show it? Are you engaging the employee or fostering disengagement?

Compassionate leadership starts with positive thoughts. The second you go negative, thinking "he/she did it on purpose," you are not on the compassionate path!

Are Your Emotions Driving the Car?
Separate the Person from the Issue

Imagine driving down the highway, minding your own business, and singing to the radio; suddenly, a car cuts you off. Do you believe the other driver did it on purpose? Are you angry? Do you follow the car and cut them off? The results, especially today, can be deadly. The same is true in the office. When someone triggers an emotional reaction in you — the report is late; it is sloppy; they are always late — the results could also be catastrophic. A recent study in collaboration with Boston Consulting Group found that work relationships, both with superiors and colleagues, are critical for employee engagement and happiness. They identified the top 25 factors for employee happiness (www.bcgperspectives.com/ Images/Global_Talent_Oct_2014_tcm80-175159.pdf, p. 16). The top five factors are: (1) Appreciation for your work; (2) Good relationships with colleagues; (3) Good work/life balance; (4) Good relationships with superiors; and (5) Company financial stability.

If you are leading with negative emotions, those emotions are driving the car; someone is going to get hurt. Finding the right mindset requires taking a pause, and recognizing when you are emotionally triggered. Anyone need a QTIP?

Tools and Strategies: QTIP Problem-Solving

A Q-tip®: The everyday, ear-cleaning, wax-remover cotton swab, also represents a tool of choice to prevent emotional leadership. In this context, QTIP stands for Quit Taking It Personally (*The Sherpa Guide*, p. 138). Seriously! Go to the store and buy as many Q-tips® as you can fit in your closet and take out a few. Hold them in your hand and repeat after me: Quit Taking It Personally. QTIP is the tool most leaders tell me is the best weapon they have against becoming emotionally charged in the workplace. The key is to separate the person from the issue and to know when you are leading with your emotions.

For example, imagine you are in a meeting; another team member interrupts you, disagrees with you or — worst yet — challenges you. Do you a) shut down; b) feel the person is doing it deliberately and defend yourself by getting angry, loud or something akin to any of these responses; or c) take a breath and not respond?

If your answer is "c," you may not need the QTIP; for everyone else, the QTIP serves as a reminder not to take it personally. Q: Quit. T: Taking. I: It. P: Personally. It's natural to feel a sting when someone interrupts you if they do it in a way that seems rude or disrespectful. What is not compassionate is reacting with your emotions.

Here are several key strategies for success:

- Pause, and check-in with yourself. Ask, "Am I taking things personally?" "Is it really about me?"

- Instead of reacting emotionally, when you find your negative emotions in the driver's seat, ask a question. For example, "Can you say more about that idea?" "What challenges do you see?" "Is the issue this or that?"

- Separate the person from the issue. What is the issue? Validate your assumptions with facts vs. emotions. Ask for clarification rather than automatically assuming negative intent. When we lead with our emotions — for example, if we think "he just says that because he does not want to do the extra work" — we are letting personalities, not issues, take the lead. Instead, focus on issues and problem-solving, not personalities.

- "QTIP will help you stay in the moment and not take things personally" (*The Sherpa Guide*, p. 139). Hold the QTIP in your pocket; paste it on your computer. From this day forward, let the QTIP remind you not to take things personally and to focus on issues not personalities.

Let's Get Personal: Our Blind Spots

An unquestioned belief provides us an opportunity to identify how our thoughts are holding us back or are keeping us in place. A better understanding of ourselves creates opportunities to support a more compassionate and engaged workforce.

Some examples of negative thoughts that I have heard in my consulting practice include:

- "They" are lazy.

- No one cares about getting the job done.

- It's not possible ("for them") to change.
- He/she is behaving that way on-purpose.

♥ *What beliefs may be holding you back from being a more compassionate leader? When we understand both our strengths and our blind spots, we can better manage ourselves, our businesses, our results and most important, we can be more empathetic and compassionate at work.*

Leading with Compassion, Building Engagement and Accountability

Compassionate leaders focus forward, looking for ways to "make things better." Compassionate leaders understand two keys: 1. That relationships drive results, build collaborative actions and support happiness at work. 2. That compassion without accountability is like dancing a tango alone. You can do it, but the tango is better with a partner who is in-step and sharing the dance with you!

These are five key things you can do to be a more compassionate leader at work, enabling you to build engagement and support your direct reports' accountability

1. **QTIP! Quit Taking It Personally!** Need I say more?
2. **Employee Engagement: Get to Know Your Employees.** There is a saying in the coaching world that, "people don't care how much you know, until they know how much you care." Compassionate leadership requires caring about your employees; and compassionate leadership requires relationship-building. How do you accomplish this?
    - Check-in regularly with your employees.
    - Get to know the strengths as well as the weaknesses of the people who report to you.

- Write accomplishments in stone. For example, share employee accomplishments, and use failures as learning opportunities.
- Support your people in being successful.

Studies consistently show that the best motivation for employees is not money — although money is always appreciated — but time and recognition from one's supervisor. In a landmark experiment called the "Hawthorne Effect," researchers at Western Electric's factory at Hawthorne in a Chicago suburb were studying the impact of working conditions on productivity; specifically, they focused on the impact of light on worker productivity. Researchers unexpectedly found that productivity increased and absenteeism decreased when supervisors spent time with their employees. Experimenters discovered that it was not the working conditions — specifically lights, whether bright or dimmer — that impacted motivation or employee productivity, but rather, "it was the fact that someone was actually concerned about their workplace, and the opportunities this gave them to discuss changes before they took place" ("The Hawthorne Effect," *The Economist*, www.theeconomist.com/node/12510632#). Showing interest and concern for your employees has consistently been shown to both improve productivity and engagement.

3. **Embrace Compassion.** Regularly focus on employee's positive accomplishments. There is a parable about the wind and the sun arguing about who was stronger. "Ok," said the sun. "I know how we can find out. Let's see who could get the man walking down the road to remove his coat first." The wind said, "I can do it faster than you." So, the wind huffed and puffed and the winds swirled fiercely around the man. The harder the wind blew, the stronger the man wrapped his coat around himself.

The sun, watching this, said, "I have a better solution." The sun shined brighter upon the man. As the sun shone, the man unbuttoned his coat, and at the end of the road, he removed his coat, placing it over his arm. The sun looked at the wind smugly and said, "I win!"

Remember, you get more with honey (or sunshine). Treat people kindly, with support and compassion. Look for opportunities to support people "to be better."

4. **Accountability Is Key!** Don't look away when someone is not doing their job. Don't do their job for them. Be a compassionate leader by insisting that your employees be accountable for what is expected of them. A client of mine was frustrated that his employee was not doing their job. The supervisor had taken away the employee's bonus and salary increases, and had frequent, frustrating discussions with them about performance; still the job was not getting done! My client started doing the employee's job.

   Instead of focusing on what the employee was not doing, I asked my client to find out what the employee cared about. After some discussion, he identified something that mattered to the employee: leaving early on Fridays. He also spent time delivering clear expectations, making time for weekly meetings and not taking his employee's behavior personally. Guess what happened? The employee started doing her job and my client was no longer doing the employee's job! Was it the carrot, spending weekly time with the employee or holding her accountable or all of the above? This leader showed compassionate leadership, that included employee accountability, building a relationship and positive reinforcement and the results speak for themselves!

   A compassionate leader understands that when you take on someone else's job, whether because you think you can do it better or because you think they will not get the job done, the outcome is the same: a disengaged, unmotivated employee is born.

5. **Compassion Is a Mindset. Fake It Until You Make It/Check-Ins.**
   Even if you believe taking time to get to know your employees
   personally is a waste of time, try it! Focus on compassion. Create
   a check-in spreadsheet. List your direct reports' names and record
   each time you check-in with each individual. Over time, you will
   notice who you are seeing more frequently, and who you might be
   avoiding. Do you have favorites, as evidenced by the frequency of
   your check-ins? Alternatively, do you focus on your "problem children" more than your high-performers?

   Next, identify things your direct reports are doing well. Write down
   their accomplishments to remind you the next time you are not
   feeling compassion. Schedule lunches, team celebrations, and find
   opportunities to embrace people where they are. Notice when you are
   being compassionate, and pat yourself on the back!

One More for Good Measure. Ditch the 80/20 Rule.

Do you believe that if 80 percent of your folks think you walk on water,
you don't need to worry about the 20 percent who don't? Wrong! Your
job as a leader, a compassionate leader, is to lead all your people, and
not just the 80 percent. The minute you look away from those folks in
the 20 percent — who also rely on you — you are not leading! It is your
job to take actions to support employee development, engagement and
productivity at work. Do you want results? Be compassionate. What if
you went to a restaurant and only 80 percent of the food tasted good?
What if only 80 percent of the cars coming off the assembly line worked
— would you want to own one of the 20 percent that was not working?
A compassionate leader is not "ok" when 20 percent of his or her
employees are disengaged.

The bottom-line is that leading with compassion requires self-reflection, adopting an attitude of inquiry, holding people accountable, and not taking things personally. Sounds easy, right? It is … if you take the time to practice daily actions of compassion, build positive relationships, heal negative ones, hold a mirror to yourself and know that dancing together is better than dancing alone!

About the Author

Laurie Copperman-Friedman, MA

Laurie is founder and President/CEO of Strategic Business Consulting, an independent consulting firm that provides both strategic and tactical tools to enhance leadership development and improve organization, team, and individual performance. She holds a Master's Degree in Human Resources and Organization Development from The George Washington University; is a certified facilitator for Myers-Briggs Type Indicator, DISC and Action Learning; and is a published author on topics including employee onboarding, retention and engagement.

A certified executive coach, change strategist and business consultant, Laurie has nearly two decades of experience working with organizations to design and develop strategies that improve business results. Her clients range from senior-level executives to line managers coming from diverse organizations including numerous non-profit organizations.

Friedman is a results-focused business coach, trainer and facilitator with a proven track record. She is known for effectively partnering with

C-level executives to improve personal effectiveness and team alignment. She incorporates a high-touch, targeted, and facilitative approach to leadership development training, business coaching, change strategies, and strategic thinking. She has designed, developed and delivered dozens of high-impact leadership development programs ranging from new supervisor and creative leadership training, to conflict management and team-building workshops.

In 2015, Laurie was awarded the Sherpa Coach of the Year award in recognition of mastery and advancement of Sherpa Coaching (www.sherpacoaching.com).

Friedman's focus on compassionate leadership has led her to develop tools and strategies to help leaders learn to not take things personally and have a more positive attitude at work.

Learn more and contact Laurie:
Laurie@sbcstrategy.com
www.SBCstrategy.com
Twitter.com/laurie10F
LinkedIn/in/Laurie-Friedman-0abb11

Chapter 4

♥

Angela Hurd Greer

"Compassion: The Logical Choice for Business"

I'm in the bathroom crying my eyes out. I'm in my late 20s, and I have a new boss. She's never been a boss before. And she requires me to account for every single minute of my day.

Literally. I keep a log.

For every task, I have to record how long it takes me. If I walk away from my desk, I have to write that down. Every meeting. Every phone call.

I'm a salaried, corporate employee. As part of my position, I lead a cross-functional, national team of leaders from across the company. And yet, she makes me write down every single minute of every single day, including this moment in the bathroom. Of course, I won't tell her I'm in here crying.

I'm angry. I'm frustrated. And frankly, I'm embarrassed. I mean, we all have days where we really don't want people to know how long it takes us in the bathroom!

This was a very stressful situation. Day in and day out: stress, stress, stress.

How do you think my overall performance would have compared if I had been working in a less stressful environment?

Logically, it makes sense that, if a person is under this kind of daily stress, his performance will suffer. This is not the type of environment where someone would thrive and flourish, rising to be his best self.

As much headway as has been made in the corporate world through leadership development, performance assessments, strategic and succession planning, soft skills training and more, in the end, people are people. There are still managers who fear that showing kindness and consideration will make them appear weak. There are also still C-suite leaders who believe that keeping employees under pressure makes them more productive. More often than not, these are the leaders who create and foster a culture of fear.

The Results Are In

The effects of work-related stress have been shown in study after study. On an individual level, stress impacts the employee physically, emotionally, intellectually and behaviorally. Physical problems can include insomnia and restless sleep; headaches and migraines; diminished or increased appetite; increased blood pressure; and lethargy, among many other symptoms. Emotional issues might present as overreacting in situations; withdrawal from communication or other interactions; or crying and sadness.

Stress can impact an individual's intellectual capacity, clouding judgment and decreasing one's ability to think clearly and make sound decisions. Behavior is also affected by stress; often tardiness and absenteeism can start to become a problem. The individual may be more prone to emotional outbursts; he may even begin to abuse alcohol or drugs.

On an organizational level, these issues become more widespread, especially if the work-related stress is a systemic problem. If you have an entire team of individuals who are dealing with stress symptoms, then their restless sleep, lethargy and sadness could translate to low morale and burnout for the whole group. If work-related stress spreads across enough teams, then it will result in an undeniable impact on the company's absenteeism and turnover rates.

As individuals deal with these physical, emotional, intellectual and behavioral symptoms, the company will face increased healthcare costs, higher accident rates and incident reports, poor performance, and lowered productivity.

The bottom line is that work-related stress negatively affects the company's bottom line.

Let's look at a real-life example: an employee calls in sick. Not even considering variations in company sick leave policies, let's only look at the interaction between the person who is ill and the person they are reporting the illness to. There is a wide spectrum of possibility for how this conversation might go.

At one end of the spectrum, Employee Mark calls Supervisor Bill:

> **Employee Mark:** *Hey Bill, I'm not going to make it in today. I'm sick.*

> **Supervisor Bill:** *Aw, sorry to hear that Mark. Is there anything you need? Is there anything we can do to help? What do we need to cover for you while you are out? Can I bring you some hot soup? You just take care of you. We hope you are feeling better soon!*

At the other end of the spectrum is Employee Chris and Supervisor Jay's interaction:

Employee Chris: Uh, Jay? This is Chris. I'm really sorry, but I'm sick today and I can't make it in. I've got a 102-degree fever and a sore throat.

Supervisor Jay: Well, Chris, you know how busy we are right now. I'm wondering if you could come in anyway. Just don't talk to anybody. I really need you in your seat.

Now consider that you wake up one morning not feeling well. You know you should call your boss to let him know you won't be coming in. How do you feel? How do you expect the call to go? Will he be concerned and accommodating? Or would you expect him to be cold, uncaring and focused only on business impacts?

Statistically speaking, your feelings are likely to be somewhere in the middle. But, imagine you are at the extreme negative end of the spectrum; put yourself in Chris's shoes.

Before you even pick up the phone to call your supervisor, Jay, you already know how it's going to go, right? You work with Jay every day. It is probably the stress from your daily interactions that made you sick in the first place. Now that you are sick, and you know you must call him, you feel even worse.

Maybe, you think, "I should just go into work anyway, because I just don't want to deal with him this morning." But no, you are too sick, and you know it's the right thing to stay home; you're probably contagious! So, you reluctantly make the call.

As you can probably tell, merely being in this situation adds even more stress on top of being ill. This could be further compounded if you, like Chris, are an hourly-employee with no sick leave benefits; you, like other hourly workers, are worried about lost wages.

Consider the perspective of the owner of the company or the Human Resources department: Would you really want Chris to come in? Would it be in the company's best interest for him to possibly infect other employees? How productive can he be while he is sick? How will it affect morale and productivity for the people who sit near him or who need to interact with him throughout the day? What impression will he make on the customers and outside vendors he works with while he is sick?

Let's compare Chris's situation to our first example, Mark. Would Mark be worried or stressed about calling his supervisor in the same the way that Chris would be? Assuming all other things are equal, which of the two employees is more likely to heal and return to work faster?

The Anecdote

This is not to imply that all stress is bad (it's not), or that there aren't other factors that cause work-related stress besides interpersonal relationships with our co-workers. But, the stress of the work that needs to be done — in the time that it needs to be done — is lessened when the burden is shared across multiple people who are working together and who are not adding to the stress through their interactions with one another.

How is that possible? People are people, aren't they? There are bound to be disagreements. There will be personality conflicts; there will be misunderstandings, unmet expectations and shortcomings. However, these stresses can all be handled by implementing just one thing: compassion.

Compassion makes us feel good, helps us heal, and even makes us more attractive. Who wouldn't want to enjoy these side effects? In the workplace, compassion has been shown to contribute to:

- Job satisfaction
- Less burnout
- Company loyalty

- Accountability for performance
- Less absenteeism
- Improved teamwork
- Lower health care costs.

With results like these, a culture of compassion would seem to be the logical choice for any organization. Oh, but how to create a culture of compassion?! You cannot coerce anyone into being compassionate.

The idea is to inspire employees to be the change they want to see in their workplace. That is, for them to create (and to want to create) an environment where everyone feels heard, respected and valued.

This can't be done by simply rolling out a new initiative or program. For an organization that sees the value in creating a compassionate culture, one step it can take is to review company policies and practices to scrutinize where compassion may be lacking, and to identify where more compassionate structures can be put in place.

♥   *Compassionate structures alone still will not change the hearts and minds of the men and women in the organization. Compassion is an inside job.*

Each party must look within and notice what needs changing. As the company leads by example in creating a more compassionate workplace, it is the goal to encourage and support its employees to do the same. A culture of compassion must be cultivated, nurtured and allowed to develop organically — one person at a time.

When you arrive at work in the morning, which version of you shows up? Is it the one who snaps at your co-worker in the break room? "Mornin,' Bill," you grumble. "You don't want to talk to me yet. I haven't had my first cup of coffee. Everybody knows not to bother me until I've had my coffee."

Or, are you the one who shows up bright and enthusiastic, sharing your joy with your co-workers? "Hey, Bill!," you say. "Good morning. I'm excited about our meeting today. I can't wait to share some ideas with you. See you at noon!" Whichever one you are, positive or negative, it's contagious. We feed off each other's energy. Be part of the solution; begin by being inspired and inspiring others.

So, What's a Person to Do?

You're feeling inspired. Now what? Cultivating compassion happens from the inside out. These are the four steps to developing yours.

1. **Always do your best, and know your best changes every day.** Some days we are up, and some days we are down. Some days we wake up rested and feeling great; other days, not so much. On those days that you aren't feeling your best, don't compare yourself or your results to those past days when you were. Just accept and acknowledge where you are in the present, and do the best you can from there.

2. **Practice self-compassion.** Don't beat up on yourself. Let go of the shoulda's, too. If you are doing the best you can on a given day, then there's nothing else you should be doing. If you were talking to your best friend, you would cut them a break. You would tell them to go easy on themselves. Show yourself the same courtesy, kindness and compassion. Know that it may be hard to get used to at first, so practice, practice, practice.

3. **Practice forgiveness.** Sometimes you will disappoint yourself. Sometimes you will disappoint others. And they will disappoint you. The word forgiveness typically implies that one person (the wronged) is "higher" than the other (the wrong-doer). This unequal footing

is deceiving. The fact is, there is no one who hasn't done something that upset another at some point in his life. And there is no one who won't be hurt or upset by another. This is universal to every single human being. So, why are we surprised by these situations? More peace comes from accepting that this is just a fact of life. This is simply how it is.

Instead of requiring someone to ask for forgiveness, instead of holding yourself at a higher level than someone who you feel wronged you, and instead of complaining or reliving whatever it was that they did, just forgive them from the standpoint of having peace in your life and moving on. You would want the same if the tables were turned (and they will be).

4. Show you care. Show you care about yourself and others. First, you. On airplanes, they don't say to put the oxygen mask on yourself first for no reason. If you don't take good care of you, then you won't be around to give to anybody else. Buy flowers for yourself. Make time for a long bath. Take a walk, read a book, go for a meandering drive, or do whatever other little thing brings you joy and that you never take time to do. Then, find ways to show others that you care. Asking about someone's day, or smiling as you pass them in the hallway are simple and effective ways to do this. Offer help on their project. Support their ideas in a meeting. Check on them when they've had a tough time. Often, it's easy to not think of our co-workers as people because we begin to see them as the function they do. Wake yourself up to remember to see others as the whole person, and then remember to treat them as the whole person too. The secret to this step is that the better you treat yourself, the better you will treat others.

When you consider all the positive outcomes that result from compassion in the workplace (job satisfaction, reduced burnout, increased company loyalty, lower healthcare costs and more), it makes good business sense. It is simply the logical choice. The challenge is to remember to be compassionate (and patient) throughout the process of cultivating a culture of compassion.

About the Author

Angela Hurd Greer, CTACC, RMT, CLYT, RYT

Energy Health Coach Angela Hurd Greer, Founder of MyLife Strategic LLC, is out to change the world — one deep belly-breath at a time.

A recovering "workaholic" and former Monday-morning panic attack sufferer, Angela works with individuals and organizations to create custom wellness solutions. She teaches strategies for managing stress and improving overall health and well-being by making small, sustainable adjustments that take only minutes per day.

With more than 20 years of leadership, consulting and training experience, Angela provides keynote speeches, seminars and workshops across a variety of organizations, including hospitals, Fortune 500 corporations, healthcare organizations, churches, senior centers, and schools. She has also held roles in corporate communications and marketing.

Angela is an interfaith minister and spiritual coach who is focused on holistic health and spiritual care. She is a multi-disciplinary holistic health practitioner and trainer, and offers a range of non-medical health and wellness solutions for organizations and individuals. She also is a former consultant to the U.S. Army Casualty Program, where for four years she trained Army staff and soldiers in this global program, and provided direct support to the families of fallen soldiers.

Learn more and contact Angela:
angela@mylifestrategic.com
www.mylifestrategic.com
502-3-LIVING (502-354-8464)

Chapter 5

♥

Lyle S. Hanna

"Servant Leadership: A Legacy"

"To whom much is given, much will be required."
— Luke 12:48 —

My dad, The Rev. Dr. Charles Morton Hanna, Jr., provided ministry, guidance and leadership to 56 Presbyterian churches predominately located in small, rural communities in the foothills of the Appalachian Mountains. As soon as I was old enough to drive, I chauffeured him on Sundays as he traveled to various congregations. Most of the towns we visited were economically challenged. Substandard housing was commonplace in many of these areas, and running water was a scarce commodity. Even though these church families often lacked basic necessities, they were eager to share whatever they had as they welcomed us into their homes and churches.

On our return, my father and I would talk about the day and pray for the congregations we visited. Often, he would share life lessons and quote scripture. Forty years later, one verse still resonates with me: "To whom much is given, much will be required," (Luke 12:48). My father's ministry gave him the chance to travel across the southeast United States, and befriend people from across the country and the globe.

No matter how busy he was, Dad was always looking to make an even bigger impact on the communities he served and within the church. The lessons I learned from my dad on the backroads of the Appalachian Mountains are the core values that drive my business and my life today.

Like my father, I, too, have been afforded many great opportunities in my career. Upon graduating from The College of Wooster in Ohio, I worked for the city human resource department in my hometown of Lexington, Kentucky. Within two years, I began an eight-year stint working for Texas Instruments, in three different states, in jobs ranging from an international compensation manager to the head of HR Compliance and Equal Employment Opportunity and Affirmative Action for the United States. I then returned home to Kentucky to work for Jerrico, the parent company for Long John Silver's and Fazoli's, and then for a Fortune 500 international company, William M. Mercer, as a human resource consultant working with business leaders dedicated to creating better workplaces for their employees.

Now, with my own human resource consulting firm, Hanna Resource Group, I work every day to improve the lives of my employees, clients, our local and state community, as well as the global community. Servant leadership is a pillar of HRG; serving the needs of others first is a core value that drives the way we do business. Our employees approach each day as an opportunity to impact the lives of others for the better. Whether we are helping someone find a more successful and fulfilling job, or providing advice to a company so that they can grow to create more opportunities for their employees, we are always focused on making a positive impact. This commitment to serve has generated a very profitable business that, in turn, enables us to do even more good work in the community. I would argue that operating a business from such a place of servitude and compassion is exactly what drives our success, and what can drive yours too.

From the moment I stepped out of the car with my dad at age 16 — and likely well before that — I knew I would use the blessings God gave to compassionately and humbly serve others. I have come to do so by following these key principles of what I now call servant leadership:

1. Serve others first

2. Make a big impact

3. Do all things with humility

4. Build your foundation on faith.

Serve Others First

♥ *Choosing others before yourself is a simple concept. Whether it's supporting the growth of your employees, giving to clients or serving the community, choosing to serve others before oneself leads to better business opportunities, larger profits and greater opportunities to serve.*

Servant leadership begins with serving those closest to you. When I opened my firm, I knew that the success of my business would be measured by the success of my employees. Therefore, I work every day to ensure I have the right people in the right positions with the right tools and talents to be successful. As company president, my job is to inspire my team and equip employees with the needed resources to best serve our clients; when the business is successful, I ensure my employees are rewarded for their dedication and hard work. I engage employees by supporting them in their personal and professional endeavors, and by taking a genuine interest in their well-being, goals and accomplishments.

To reward other employers for their dedication in supporting and engaging employees, I partnered with the Kentucky Society of Human

Resource Management (SHRM) and the Kentucky Chamber of Commerce to create the Kentucky Best Places to Work program. This program recognizes the top 100 best places to work in the Commonwealth of Kentucky. To make this list, employees provide anonymous feedback about their workplaces, identifying their company as an employer of choice in the bluegrass state. The prestigious honor of being named a Kentucky Best Places to Work organization helps companies attract stronger candidates, provides marketing opportunities and helps increase workforce engagement.

One of the reasons I founded the Best Places to Work program is to recognize the fact that every great business is only as successful its employees; human capital has immense value in every type of business. Often, my company is asked to stabilize an organization in turmoil and change company culture to ultimately drive company profit and growth. We find that the companies most in need of assistance often lack strong leadership, a developed human resource function and/or a compassionate workplace.

Recently, Hanna Resource Group partnered with a manufacturer in desperate need of both strategic HR-leadership and an engaging, open and accepting workplace culture. This organization had the capital and market to expand rapidly; due to the culture, however, it was failing to attract and retain talent. Our team stabilized the organization and opened dialogue with employees so the business could expand and meet its financial goals. Within weeks, we brought optimism to this company and significantly improved internal communications. We initiated conversations and developed relationships with every employee. We also instituted focus groups and an employee engagement survey; based upon their feedback, we made immediate improvements to the organization. The more we serve our employees, the more employees are encouraged to give to the organization, thereby increasing employee engagement, satisfaction and, ultimately, increased profits.

Another client with similar circumstances was amazed by the impact that a servant leadership culture can have on employees. This healthcare organization of more than 50 employees was the most dysfunctional business we had encountered. The company's president had mismanaged and abused the organization since its inception. The organization's leadership team lacked the training and tools they needed to perform, and the company's employees often compared their day at work to a day in a war zone: "explosive and catastrophic, but if we stick together, we — and the company — might survive."

The company's owner called us in to assess the challenges and formulate a solution to the myriad problems he was facing. Within days of partnering with this company, we had removed and replaced the company president, and met with each employee to triage their concerns. Within 30 days, we doubled the size of the organization through acquisition. Even though the culture was still unstable, we rallied employees' support and engagement. Through our guidance, the company committed to provide a compassionate workplace to serve employees. One year later, the company had completely rebranded itself and was earning sustainable profits. Today, the organization is experiencing double-digit growth and long-tenured employees are heavily vested in the company's success.

The successes of our clients and, in turn, our business, provide me and our employees the opportunities to have a bigger impact within our community. For example, I choose to give my time and talent to the Society of Human Resource Management (SHRM) and Habitat for Humanity. As the founder, past and current president of the Kentucky Habitat for Humanity, and a former chair of the SHRM Foundation, I want my legacy to be that of a visionary servant leader who makes big plans, and who has the support of family, friends and faith to accomplish seemingly impossible goals.

Make a Big Impact — Hammering in the Hills

Another lesson I had learned from my dad in pursuit of servant leadership was to commit to big projects — big enough that they require your friends, family and faith to complete. Kentucky's largest Habitat build was a 1997 project where, in a tent in Vác, Hungary, with U.S. President Carter, we committed our state to build 50 houses in Kentucky in just one week, a project we named "Hammering in the Hills." At that time, few states had come close to building 50 houses within a year, let alone within a week. True to my dad's lesson, building 50 houses in a week certainly required the help and support of my family, a lot of friends and a lot of faith. Later, we successfully built a Habitat home in less than 24 hours.

I have always been inspired by the saying, "Make no small plans. Only big plans have the power to kindle people's imagination and drive them to great results." Each project I led with Kentucky Habitat for Humanity seemed impossible at the outset; often even Millard Fuller, the founder and former president of Habitat for Humanity International, questioned our ability to succeed in what seemed like impossible tasks. I've found that, with encouragement and optimism, people really do rally around lofty goals and big ideas.

Do All Things with Humility

My dad taught me to make big plans and tackle impossible tasks, but he also showed me that the way to accomplish Goliath tasks is through humility. We learn to make big plans and strive for big goals, but to do so without big egos. Servant leadership shows our employees, our clients and the people who we interact with daily that we have a willingness to help others to be successful, and that we must be careful not to let our egos become stumbling blocks.

It is important to remember that, sometimes, to accomplish the biggest goal and conquer the biggest opportunity, we must be willing to help in the smallest capacity. Our willingness to help in all situations and at all levels of service builds strong relational bonds between family members, co-workers and community. We're not just checking accomplishments off a list, highlighting our "good deeds;" we are making real impact on others' lives whether it is by providing them a satisfying and fulfilling job or building a house for a person in need.

Build Your Foundation in Faith

Last but not least, my father taught me to keep faith at the center of everything I do. Since I began my business in 2007, we've opened each team meeting with prayer, asking God to use us in the best way possible to serve our clients and our community. We are a Christian business, and I encourage employees to bring their faith to work. Prayer is a good way of keeping in touch with the spiritual side of life. Even for non-faith-based businesses, it can be vital to build your foundation and your practices on deeply held beliefs in the value of community, connection, abundance and opportunity, or servitude to customers and other stakeholders.

Each day I pray for insight and for God to place in my path the people whose lives or businesses can be enhanced by the services HRG provides. I know I can have the greatest impact overall when my business is financially successful so that I have no hesitation to pray for healthy and profitable client work. This prayer manifests itself in opportunities to solve HR and business problems such as hiring great people or building "Best Places to Work." It also creates opportunities to solve community problems such as helping Habitat for Humanity build more houses in Kentucky and around the world, or assisting the United Way in their fundraising efforts to improve the lives of local citizens.

At the time, I never realized that the discussions I had with my dad while traveling on the backroads of Eastern Kentucky would afford me with so many life lessons and opportunities — personally and professionally. I am truly humbled by the opportunities that God has given me to serve and hope that the spirit of servant leadership inspires others to create better places for people to work and live.

About the Author

Lyle S. Hanna, SPHR, SHRM-SCP

Lyle is the President and CEO of Hanna Resource Group (HRG), which focuses on innovative business and human resource strategy. Lyle's experience includes: Managing Director for the Compensation, Benefits & Retirement Group division for Palmer & Cay; Principal and Global Business Development Consultant for William M. Mercer, Inc.; Director of Human Resources for Jerrico, Inc.; and Manager, Corporate Human Resources at Texas Instruments.

Lyle uses his 40 years of experience in corporate human resource management to assist
clients with strategic design and implementation of a wide range of programs, including
retirement, health, compensation systems and
general human resource planning.

Lyle has served in various key roles within the
Society for Human Resource Management
(SHRM) since the late 1980s, and has served
twice as Chair of the Kentucky SHRM State
Council. Lyle is a former Chair of the national
SHRM Foundation's Board of Directors. In 2005, Kentucky SHRM
established an award called the Lyle Hanna Spirit Award to recognize
other volunteers who give mightily of their time and talent to the human
resource profession.

Lyle's extensive professional service includes his former role as Chair of
the Kentucky Chamber of Commerce, his founding of the Best Places to
Work in Kentucky program and his service to the Lexington Rotary and
the United Way of the Bluegrass in Lexington, KY.

Lyle has been deeply involved in the expansion of Habitat for Humanity
into 100+ countries around the globe. He is the former Vice Chair of
the Habitat for Humanity International Board of Directors and Chair
of the Habitat Global Leadership Council. He also served on the Global
Development Committee to help raise $3.9 billion. Lyle currently serves
as the Chair of the Development Committee for Lexington Habitat and
was the founder and original chair of Kentucky Habitat for Humanity.
He once again now Chairs Kentucky Habitat for Humanity and is
helping to drive a major initiative — to be completed in 2020 — through
which the organization will build 1,000 houses.

Lyle is a graduate of the College of Wooster with a BA in Urban Studies (Economics/Political Science). In 1992, he achieved lifetime certification as a Senior Professional in Human Resources (SPHR) and is a SHRM Senior Certified Profession in HR.

Learn more and contact Lyle:
Lyle@hannaresources.com
859-514-7724

Chapter 6

♥

Paula H. Harvey

"Demonstrating Compassion at Work Through Effective Mentoring"

One of the most compassionate ways HR can assist employee development is by planning, coordinating and establishing an effective mentorship program. This is not the easiest task, as it takes strong intention and dedication with support from executive management to make a program like this successful.

When I had my consulting agency, many of my clients asked me to help them establish a mentoring program. In my initial appointment with the client, I would ask them very pointedly why they wanted to set one up. If it was because their boss was on the golf course and heard that it was a good idea, I became very suspicious about whether the program would have strong "top-down" support. If, instead, they told me that they wanted to invest in their employees and grow their high-potential staff, I was excited to help them.

Throughout my career, I have had the amazing privilege of mentoring some of the finest HR professionals to achieve their potential. They usually, in turn, have reverse-mentored me and have made me a better HR leader. I have also been guided by some wonderful business mentors during my career. For 17 years, I have been teaching the SHRM

Learning System for HR certifications. When we discuss the section on leadership, I always ask my students — by show of hands — if they have a coach in their current job and/or a mentor for future jobs and their career. Woefully, over the years, very few hands have gone up. I usually chastise my students and tell them that having a mentor is a key to success in business. Bill Gates has Warren Buffet as a lifelong mentor. Sir Richard Branson has Sir Freddie Laker. They both understand that going it alone is foolhardy when it is so much easier to have a guide.

> *"If you ask any successful businessperson, they will always [say they] have had a great mentor at some point along the road."*
>
> — **Sir Richard Branson** —

What is a Mentor?

A mentor should be a trusted counselor or teacher who has a significant impact on their mentee's work life (and possibly personal life too). My first mentor, Dr. Andre Lefevre, was a guiding light who would call out me on my stuff. He never told me what I had to do; instead he gave me lots of suggestions and helped me to make decisions that were critical to my professional success. He died of cancer at the early age of 50, but I hear his voice in my head throughout my career every time I have made important work decisions.

My first mentor taught me that life is a cycle of ups and downs; I should always make choices that I can live with ethically and happily. He taught me to strive to be the best I can be in my profession, and to not settle for mediocrity. One of the biggest lessons that I learned was to pay it forward. Because I was fortunate to have a great mentor, I strive to be a good one to others. Andre encouraged me to mentor future generations of HR professionals when I was ready. And I did!

Who are Mentors?

In the past, mentors were usually male managers in their 50s and 60s who would mentor the younger generation of workers on "how business was done" at the organization. The presumption was that the way we have always done things must be the right way. With the new century and modern electronic communications, modern mentoring has evolved beyond the tradition of a senior taking juniors under his wing.

Now, there are many kinds of mentors. Ever-changing workplace demographics demand mentors of a broader range of ages, gender, backgrounds and education levels. With recent technological advances such as cloud computing, social media and smartphones, mentors can be located half-way across the globe from their mentees.

What Do Mentors Do?

Mentors can do a variety of things for their mentees. Many mentor-mentee relationships are created organically. The mentor or the mentee usually formally asks for the relationship, or it blossoms into a mentorship with a more informal ask. A mentor's prime focus should be to support the mentee to be the best they can be and prepare them for future opportunities.

One of my current mentees met me at an HR event when she saw me looking for a place to sit. She was a college student at the time, and waved me over to come sit by her. After the event, she asked for my card and immediately found me on LinkedIn. She invited me to lunch the next week. At the lunch meeting, she point-blank asked me to be her mentor. I was so impressed by her that I had to say yes. I guided her with internships, resume writing, and was a reference for her first job out of college.

Mentoring can take many forms. Some mentors enjoy being a cheerleader and positive encourager, helping their mentee to build self-confidence and poise. Others can play the devil's advocate and constantly question their mentee's decisions. Both types of mentors challenge their mentees to be the best that they can be. The key is to genuinely care about your mentee, and help them to perform in today's changing world.

Some mentoring happens very unconsciously. A leader may give a piece of advice that will make a lifelong impact on the recipient, who becomes an "unknown" mentee. The mentee looks up to that person and wants to emulate their leadership style and decision-making processes. It is important for leaders to recognize when this is happening and to formalize the mentoring relationship.

Effective Mentoring

To make the mentorship effective, the mentee must go into the relationship leaving their ego behind and must be open to learning from their mentor. They also must challenge their mentor with thoughtful questions. The mentor must know to say they will get back with an answer if they are unsure at the time on what is best for their mentee. The mentee must learn from the lessons their mentor shares and apply that knowledge.

A mentee must adapt to their mentor's ability to help them. Some organizations might have formal programs where planned, periodic meetings are made by the mentor-mentee. This is not the norm. Most relationships are less formal, but it is key to meet often either in-person or electronically to discuss progress.

My mentees tend to either have Starbucks meetings or lunch with me once a month, especially during critical times in their careers. Others text me or use social media to keep in touch and to ask for advice. Recently, one of my mentees used Twitter to message me and other HR professionals for advice on the next step in her career. It became a two-day event that reached many folks in our sphere of Twitter followers, and hopefully helped many.

♥ *Often in a mentoring relationship, the mentor will uncover unknown abilities of their mentee. The mentor must be astute to help them grow those abilities if it will help them to be successful.*

Commonly, the mentor will encourage the mentee to acquire knowledge, skills and abilities that they might not have considered. They also will challenge their mentee to take calculated risks and pursue new opportunities to obtain useful job experience.

The Mentoring Process

This is a chart that I have used in mentor training sessions. It shows the steps of Identify, Introduce, Invest and Empower that are key to the mentoring process. This chart is gratefully borrowed from *360 Solutions*, "The Mentoring Process," 2010.

Identify. In this step, the mentee identifies the potential mentor. It is critical that the mentee believes this person will care for them in a compassionate, integrity-based and competent manner. Often, performing some type of personality testing can be very helpful to understand each other. Setting up parameters for meetings and frequency also is important. This is where expectations are created, and success is defined. Equally important is understanding what methods each person likes to use for communication. For example, all my mentees know that if they really want to talk to me quickly, that they should send a text, as that is what I will answer first. In my case, a phone message is the worst way to communicate with me.

Introduce. It is very important for the mentor to be a connector for their mentee. They should help their mentee by opening doors to help them meet others in their organization, profession or community. The mentor often gains greatly in this step as well by widening their own personal network in the process of assisting their mentee.

Mentoring Process

Empowerment & Leadership

Mentor/Mentee Personality Assessment

Relational/Technical Skill Development

Organizational Strategy & Core Ideology

Empower — Release to Perform — Integrity — Identity
Encourage — Competence
Coach — Compassion
Performing — Building Trust
Commitment — Adoption
Acceptance — Preparation
Provide Opportunities — Developing — Connecting — Organization
Practicing — Purpose
Invest — Equip for Success — Job Role — Introduce

Invest. This step involves the most time. This happens by teaching, coaching and utilizing knowledge of the mentoring process with the mentee. This takes great intention on the part of the mentor to find opportunities for their mentee. It may require asking others for their thoughts and opinions; and possibly, the mentor needs to do research to have meaningful advice for their mentee. An important outcome is developing the mentee's interpersonal skills; active listening, effective communication and conflict management skills are critical to professional success.

Empower. This stage is one of the most rewarding for the mentor — and often the most terrifying for the mentee. At some point, the mentor must release their duckling because they have become a beautiful swan. The formal part of the mentorship is usually done. Encouragement that the mentee is ready for bigger and better things is very important. True mentor/mentees are never gone, however; they are just a phone call, text message, email or prayer away.

Challenges in Mentorships

Establishing and maintaining a productive mentoring partnership is not easy. Below are several common challenges that I have witnessed in my career.

1. **Mentors can be hard to find.** Most mentors are busy professionals; time is money to them. It is important for mentees to be respectful of their mentors' time. For this reason, mentorships must be supported top-down in the organization for the mentoring program to be successful. Mentors also must be given flexibility to shape the mentorship to fit their professional style.

2. **Mentorships often fall apart.** Make goals and objectives for the mentorship. Create a mentor-mentee contract. Find ways to measure outcomes of the relationship.

3. **Mentors often do not know what to do for their mentees.** Create a training session for mentors. Further, HR should continually support mentors in their organizations.

4. **Matching the mentor to the mentee is critical.** If the mentor is not comfortable teaching others, it is not a good match. The mentor must be confident that they have something to offer their mentee and know how to communicate to them. Remember that knowledge is not always easily transferred to the mentee.

Important Mentoring Tools

The following list is from the book Mentoring by Gordon Shea, with my comments added:

1. **Shifting Context** — Encourage the mentee to think in different ways about issues they face.

2. **Listening Actively** — Listen to your mentee without passing judgment or giving answers immediately. Help them to seek solutions together. This skill is probably the most powerful tool of a mentor. It allows mentors to really understand their mentee, so that they can give them sage advice.

3. **Naming Feelings** — Use emotional intelligence to allow the mentee to express what they are feeling and to understand why they possibly need to make a change.

4. **Enabling Constructive Confrontation** — Confront issues in a non-destructive manner to keep a positive relationship with the mentee.

5. **Providing Information That Has a Positive Impact** — Mentors should share ideas, knowledge, stories, and solutions to support their professional advice; make sure that advice is useful and practical.

6. **Giving Permission** — Allow the mentee to be themselves to boost their self-confidence.

7. **Being Genuinely Concerned** — Help the mentee to look for answers beyond the obvious. Genuine curiosity provides new, and often exciting, experiences that allow the mentee to do things they never imagined.

Keys to Success for Mentoring Programs

- Obtain executive management support

- Train potential mentors on the best practices of effective mentoring

- Match mentees to mentors for best fit

- Have mentees and mentors create a mentorship contract or guidelines
  - Include frequency of meetings
  - Include ways to communicate

- Mentor and mentees must have a frank conversation on expectations of the relationship

- Set up goals and proposed outcomes

- Measure how the program is achieving its goals

- Review the program periodically

Final Thoughts

Mentoring is critical to the development of employees, as it allows the mentee to acquire business perspectives, develop strategic decision-making ability, and build leadership skills. A mentor can make a life-changing difference in assisting an employee to reach their highest potential. As an added bonus, mentoring usually helps develop mentors into better leaders. Few programs can better demonstrate compassion in the workplace than an effective mentoring program. It is a key initiative in the career development of high-potential employees.

"We make a living by what we get; we make a life by what we give."
— Winston Churchill —

Reference

Rousseau, Mata. "Structured Mentoring," presentation at SHRM 2011 Annual Conference. June 29, 2011.

About the Author

Paula H. Harvey, MBA, SHRM-SCP, SPHR, GPHR, ASC

Paula is VP of Human Resources/Safety for Schulte Building Systems in Hockley, TX. She has worked in the retail, services, construction and manufacturing industries and has 30 years' experience in Human Resources. Paula earned her Bachelors of Business Administration in International Marketing and Operations Management from the University of Texas at Austin, and earned her MBA with a concentration in HR Management from the University of North Carolina at Charlotte. She also has doctoral studies in leadership.

As a Senior Global Certified Professional of Human Resources and Safety, Paula teaches business and leadership-related topics tailored to working professionals. She is an internationally recognized speaker on global and strategic business issues, has published and has been quoted in articles on HR topics, and is the co-author of two HR-related books and several articles.

Harvey is an active member of the Society for Human Resources Management (SHRM) serving on the SHRM Talent Acquisition Panel and has served as the SE Membership Advisory Council Representative

(MAC), NCSHRM State Director/President and President of Union County HR Association and Charlotte Area SHRM. In 2018, she will begin serving on the board of the SHRM Foundation.

She is a past recipient of NCSHRM HR Professional of the Year and NCSHRM HR Humanitarian of the Year awards. Since moving back to Texas in 2015, Paula is a member of HR Houston, where she mentors students as a member of the University Liaison committee. Notably, she is proud to be a lifetime Girl Scout, a 22-year Red Cross volunteer, and holds two martial arts black belts.

Learn more and contact Paula:
Paulah@sbslp.com
Twitter.com/Paula4Harvey
LinkedIn.com/in/paulaharvey

Chapter 7

♥

Michelle Hollingshead

"Opening the Dialogue: Do We Really Value Diversity of Thought and How Compassion Can Help"

With recent cases, such as the firing of an employee after the leak of the controversial Google memo questioning the company's diversity practices, the reaction to a professor questioning policy at Evergreen State College and his refusal to participate in the "day of absence/presence," and the CEO of Facebook posting a defense of a board member's support of the Republican presidential nominee as a reminder of the importance of "diversity" for the company, we are increasingly finding ourselves in this dilemma:

Do we *really* value diversity of thought?

Diversity of thought is the idea that there is more than "one way." It is one thing to say we value diversity of thought, and it is another thing to put this value into practice in the face of intense challenge to our core beliefs.

In my mid-20s, I was excommunicated from my religion. My theological doubts about there being only one "true" religion conflicted with the standards of the organization; ultimately, I was removed as a member.

Expulsion is an answer to dissension, yet what are the long-term implications of pushing opposing views or questions away and imposing silence? The impulse to expel is driven by a need to defend a position and maintain control by enforcing compliance; it is the antithesis of working to engender commitment. Yet, without sincere commitment, engagement in any pursuit — personal or professional — is limited.

What We Aspire to Takes Courage

Valuing differing perspectives and approaches is key to leveraging diversity and inclusion as an organizational resource. Research shows that when employees believe their organization is committed to — and supportive of — diversity and employees feel included, the organization reports better business performance in terms of ability to innovate, responsiveness to changing customer needs and team collaboration (Deloitte, "Waiter: Is That Inclusion in My Soup? A New Recipe to Improve Business Performance," 2013.)

♥ *When global diversity is valued and well managed, organizations can adapt to the changing needs of customers and remain relevant in an era when flexibility and innovation are essential to success.*

A workplace that embraces diversity can be powerfully productive. Each person is unique and valuable; valuing differences strengthens engagement and productivity, and reinforces the elements of a positive organizational culture. However, in practice, the potential of this resource can be difficult to manage.

What we aspire to takes courage. Imagine the courage it takes to question, challenge, and voice doubts or concerns. For example, think about a time when you challenged your boss or questioned someone in a position of authority over you. I bet it felt risky. Now imagine the

courage it takes to stop speaking and to listen; to open your heart and
mind with curiosity and humility; to hold the intention to understand
a view different from your own; to surface your assumptions; and to do
this in a way that fosters trust and mutual respect. This might also feel
risky as you open yourself to uncertainty and to the challenging of your
beliefs. While conflicting ideologies are hard to integrate, practices such
as beginning interactions with a compassionate mindset, disconnecting to
connect, opening dialogue, and participating in co-creative learning journeys can offer colleagues a path for growth and development — and are
ways to bring people together despite the tensions in our polarized world.

How a Compassionate Mindset Can Help

Compassion is defined as the emotional response we have when we
perceive suffering and choose to make an authentic effort to help.
A compassionate mindset is motivated by genuine care and concern for
others' welfare; it is remembering that we all suffer in our lives, and that
we share a longing for happiness and freedom from human suffering.

Practicing compassion in the face of opposing views involves releasing
judgments about yourself and others. Judgment is the mind's way of
creating separation. Separation breeds more separation, and typically
evolves into an "us vs. them" mindset and further entrenchment of
positions. One reflection I use to optimize my attitude toward others is
to remind myself that every single person and being, at an essential level,
is just like me. Everybody wants to be happy — just like me. Everybody
wants to avoid suffering — just like me. Even if they don't do what
I think they should, they are just like me. Even if they believe in things
I don't believe in, they are just like me. Even if they hurt others and cause
harm, they are just like me.

A mindset of compassion is one that remembers our shared humanity and discards a lens of "better than other" or "less than other" as the basis for examining differing ideas. When I listen with humility and curiosity, I remember that my truth or way of seeing isn't the truth. It is not my job to fix you or to make you see things the way I see them. The way I am seeing the world is shaped by my culture, language, biology and personal history. My assumptions and opinions are guided by these forces, as are the assumptions and opinions of others. I can begin interactions by taking personal responsibility to more consciously choose the beliefs I advocate for and the avenues I use for communication.

Disconnecting to Connect

One of the challenges to being more conscious about our interactions with others, as noted above, is the use of email, intranet sites, text messages and social media to exchange ideas. Be curious enough to consider "What would have been different if ideas had been shared and discussed in person? Could the outcome have been different?"

In a rush to advocate for our positions, and with a plethora of avenues to pump ideas out into the world, it is easy to forget the receiver and the possible impact these messages may have. Our brain continually makes assumptions based on our filters and biases, and then moves to action based on those inferences or stories. For example, as a woman, I made many assumptions about the author of the Google memo that I was unable to keep in check. Based on those assumptions, I felt annoyed and formed an opinion about him and his motives. My assumptions might be true, or they might not be. Many times, we later learn that we didn't have all the information or we misinterpreted something, and then we feel remorse for our words or actions; or, we simply look for information to confirm our beliefs and filter out the rest. This is even more pronounced when we are entrenched in our position and our ego craves the confirmation that we are right.

When dealing with highly charged positions, especially at work, I recommend disconnecting from technology as a means of engaging more thoughtfully with others. To practice exploring opposing views and move forward, it is best to bring people together face-to-face with structured formats. This is a muscle or skill that needs to be built in a proactive way in organizations so that diversity of thought can be utilized as a resource. A specific practice I would like to introduce to accomplish this is dialogue.

Opening the Dialogue

We are all subject to bias on a personal and organizational level. We cannot do away with bias, but we can become conscious of bias — our preferences — and adopt conscious attitudes that will enable us to deal with bias effectively by acknowledging it, addressing it with curiosity and humility, and generating open and transparent dialogue that can help us transcend it.

Dialogue can be used in groups or one-on-one, and is based on the following principles:

- Dialogue is a key tool for personal and organizational transformation
- Dialogue practice involves suspending judgment, listening deeply and balancing advocacy and inquiry

People share their truth and listen to the experiences of others, allowing for assumptions and beliefs to be exposed and reexamined. When using dialogue as a tool, both the sender and receiver have specific roles and responsibilities. The receiver agrees to pay focused attention, begins with a mindset of compassion and curiosity, practices suspending one's own perspective, allows the sender to have a view that is different from one's own, and exercises the capacity to contain one's own reactions. The sender agrees to talk about herself or himself and not the other person (I vs. you), offer short bits of information, keep the message focused on the topic, and check the summary to confirm whether it is accurate and, if not, to send it again more clearly.

There are three parts of a productive dialogue: the summary, validation and empathy. The summary is when the receiver paraphrases the sender's message and then asks, "Did I get it? Did I get you?" Then the receiver validates the sender by stating, "Your world makes sense to me because ..." This is the opportunity for making sense based on the experiences of the other person. The final part is demonstrating empathy by stating, "I imagine all of this would make you feel ..." This is the opportunity for the receiver to imagine the emotions of the other person based on their experiences, and then check in to see if anything was missed. The receiver does not express his or her own views or opinions until the roles are reversed.

Example

Sender: Speaks about a topic he/she desires to explore.

Receiver: Replies with, "I heard you say ...," or, "If I heard you right ... Did I get it?"

Sender: Responds "yes" or "no" or "almost," then resends the message with any part that was incorrect or missing.

Receiver: Continues reflecting, and then prompts, "Is there more?" or "Could you tell me more?"

Sender: Once the thoughts are complete and reflected upon accurately, says, "There is no more."

Receiver: The receiver has completed the steps of Summary, Validation and Empathy.

The Sender and Receiver reverse roles.

During the 2016 US election, many of my friends, family members and colleagues were struggling to be in relationships with others having differing views. This was a particularly challenging time for my husband, Dan and me. He was torn as Donald Trump was selected as the Republican presidential candidate; he ultimately chose to write his own name on the ballot. I was committed to electing our first female president. Even though we had walked together to vote in previous elections — knowing that we would cancel out each other's vote — something was different this time. Just watching the news would trigger arguments, anger and judgment.

Dan and I ended up using the practice of dialogue to help us communicate. We would meet in my office, sitting knee to knee, with our dialogue prompts to guide us and practice. Specifically, this created a way for one of us to be listened to and understood, and to discuss touchy topics without emotional reactions. This also helped us to have a clearer understanding of the other's worldview, be more critical of the information we were reading, and to cross check our sources.

While this example is deeply personal, we each bring parts of our experiences with us into the workplace, as our experiences shape our identities. The principles and practices are the same when using dialogue in an organization with groups or with facilitated learning. I will now share more about human development based on the principles of dialogue and the benefits of participating in co-creative learning journeys.

Participating in Co-Creative Learning Journeys

Co-creative learning journeys bring people in an organization together with structures and practices that enable them to learn with and from each other while focused on a shared goal or aspired future. The design is based on the premise that people grow and develop by engaging in dialogue and practicing skills together in a safe and experiential environment. Dialogue is a key tool for coming into higher-order relationships and discovering higher-order systems by accessing the wisdom that is in the collective. Due to the pace of change, complexity and interdependence of our world, learning programs where one or more people simply impart a solution are increasingly less effective.

In a recent corporate Diversity & Inclusion initiative, the participants and I used a fishbowl exercise to open dialog and explore perspectives on the perceived impact the corporate culture had on gender and leadership in the organization. The fishbowl approach begins with a circle of chairs in the middle of the room; it is an opportunity to listen to a group of colleagues having a conversation as they would have behind closed doors. The intention is to witness another group's perspective by simply listening to their conversation and without interacting.

We invited the women leaders to gather in the fishbowl to discuss three questions that reflected on their experience related to specific aspects of the organization's culture; their managers had a chance to listen and observe. Then we invited the managers to gather in the fishbowl and answer the same questions. What I noticed is that it took each group a while to begin to speak more freely about their experiences and opinions. As each group spoke more transparently, the dilemmas they faced began to surface; they exposed more of their assumptions and doubts. During a debriefing of the fishbowl exercise, the participants expressed more compassion for the experiences of their colleagues, less judgment and more openness to challenge their previously held positions.

Another exercise that is extremely powerful for opening dialogue is personal history as the root of unconscious bias. In this exercise, small groups explore the messages they received about life and work as a child and any specific message they received about gender while growing up. In small groups, each participant had the opportunity to describe a time when they experienced bias or exclusion, and to share the impact. These types of exercises create opportunities for people to share their worldview based on their personal experiences and to remember that, while our specific experiences vary, many of us have suffered, felt isolated or alone.

You might be questioning whether it's the responsibility of an organization to take time for employees to participate in compassionate practices, such as dialogue, in connection with personal and organizational transformation. I assert that, as we evolve, the workplace can become a place for ongoing developmental growth of *all* its people, more effectively leveraging diversity of thought. Many beliefs we hold about groups that are different from us are based on stories or beliefs that we inherited; we then took those beliefs as our own, ultimately creating organizational cultures based on those beliefs. Stories that further oppression are not serving future generations, and hinder us in achieving a world where all human beings have a chance to thrive.

We are being asked to question the stories we are telling and the actions we take from those positions in the workplace and beyond. When we engage in compassionate practices, where we are committed to deeper exploration of our beliefs and assumptions, we create space for all of us to grow; we expand with this support, and come together in service of building a better future.

About the Author

Michelle Hollingshead, M.Ed., PCC

Michelle Hollingshead founded Imprint in 2009 with the mission of helping individuals and organizations leave a meaningful imprint on our world. She designs and delivers leadership development programs that connect business outcomes with the human dimension of business. Michelle consults on corporate culture transformation, where she bridges gaps between people from diverse backgrounds while emphasizing human potential and consciousness.

With more than 15 years of experience in learning and development, Michelle understands that the barriers to organizational transformation are stubborn and complex. Solutions must be holistic, systemic and address long-held biases.

Michelle coaches and consults with executives, managers and teams in Fortune 500 companies, privately-held companies and in the non-profit sector. She has worked with organizations such as Cigna, Cisco Systems, Lexmark, Johnson Controls, Procter & Gamble, Nationwide Affinity Solutions, Brown-Forman, University of Kentucky, Microsoft and others.

Michelle completed her professional coach training through Coach University and is a PCC-credentialed member of the International Coaches Federation. She is a graduate of CTI's Co-Active Leadership Program. She holds a Master's of Education in Curriculum Development from Lesley University. Michelle is certified in Life Styles Inventory, Life Styles Inventory with Item Level Feedback (360), Organizational

Culture Inventory, Organizational Effectiveness Inventory, Barrett
Values Assessment and the Deliberately Developmental Organization
Assessment. She also has extensive training in yoga, meditation and
mindfulness practices.

Michelle began her career in multicultural education before transitioning
to coaching, consulting and entrepreneurship. She is an award-winning
teacher, yoga enthusiast and proud mother of two who is an avid reader
and loves to travel.

Learn more and contact Michelle:
michelle@imprintcoaching.com
www.imprintcoaching.com
LinkedIn.com/in/michellehollingshead

Chapter 8

♥

Dr. Milli McIntosh

"#AnXPOSEDHeart ... HR Style!"

"A good head and a good heart are always a formidable combination."

— Nelson Mandela —

It's amazing how multiple children from the same family can turn out so differently. And this difference can exist even when they have the same crimson blood running through their veins, were all raised in the same household, were all given the same opportunities, and all received the same love and affection. (As for that love part, my brothers and sometimes my sister would inevitably say to me, "You were always mom's favorite" of which mom would vehemently deny, and then so graciously respond, "That's not true; I love you all the same." God rest her soul ...) There are four of us — two boys and two girls. Yet, even with the familial DNA at work, children are all so different! They bring different skills, thoughts, personalities and opinions to the table. These differences among siblings bear a striking resemblance to "organizational talent" in the workplace.

Carrying the torch of the first born was an honor, or so I thought; I realized later in life it was both a blessing and a curse. A blessing in that, as the oldest, "I was in charge." That's right. Because of being #1, positional power was mine! Sound familiar? How many folks do you know who, once promoted to supervisor or manager, thought that just because they received the title, people were going to listen to them? Being the oldest was also a curse in that, ultimately, I was responsible. The buck stopped with me! Whatever decisions I made, regardless of the outcome, were all on me — negative or positive. Again, sound familiar? Good leaders realize and understand that tough decisions are made daily. Some of those decisions are made minute-by-minute. And those decisions might affect not only the leader but the organization as a whole.

Back to my siblings: according to them, I was "soft." I take too much of an interest in others' well-being. They would often say, "You always want to fix people's problems." My personal favorite is, "You care too much about others; your heart is exposed! People can see it." Growing up in the concrete jungles of Chicago, this was not a good thing. You had to be tough! Wearing a suit of armor was the expected fashion of the day. This served as personal protective equipment (PPE) so as not to be pierced or wounded by societal ills.

My daily PPE was different: GRACE and HUMILITY was the suit that protected my body and soul. I wore it proudly! But doing so did not come without heartache and ridicule. The ramblings of my siblings as it pertained to my "caring demeanor" began resonating negatively in my soul. I was truly burdened with the vibrating thoughts that perhaps something was really wrong with me. Caring for and about others is what I have always done and what I always felt. But why? Vibrating thoughts yield steady questions: "Are females more intrinsically compassionate? Perhaps that's it. It's because I am a girl? But wait, my sister is a girl and she didn't have "IT"! My brothers obviously showed no signs of "IT." Why me? Why not the others?"

To truly understand requires a journey back in time. A time when I thought I knew the meaning of true leadership. A time when I thought leadership meant power. Margaret Thatcher once said, "Power is like being a lady; if you have to tell people you are, you aren't." As an Officer in the United States Army, my power was legitimate and coercive. My power was bestowed upon me by the President of the United States because of my earned position and earned rank. Although I was proficient at performing every task I was asked to take on, and was familiar with military culture, soldiers did what I said because I had the right to give orders based on my position as an Officer; I believed it too. My skills, knowledge and disposition mattered not to them. I said, "Jump," and they replied, "Yes ma'am. How high?"

There were times the soldiers were even threatened. Once, I threatened to take a soldier's pay. Then, it was the "Army way." I was a young, freshly commissioned officer and a first-generation college grad with something to prove. My job was to get them to do what I wanted, when I wanted. Accomplish the mission! They were never asked; they were told! It didn't matter the circumstance, the situation, who, what, where, when or why. I told! As a young leader, again I was only doing what I was taught by more senior officers and senior NCOs (non-commissioned officers). The results were positive, and failure was not an option. Disciplinary issues were minimum, and almost non-existent. People worked synergistically and were extremely productive. Again, it was the Army way!

By contrast, as a member of "Corporate America," I quickly realized that the effectiveness of the leadership approach used in the military was quite ineffective on the employees of a printing company. Occasions in which people completed tasks simply because I "told" them to do so were few and far between. The use of my legitimate and coercive power was sometimes unstable, even unpredictable. Employees of this organization had their own ideas, personalities and belief systems (mimicking my siblings). Something had to change. Someone had to change. I had to change.

My leadership style had to change for me to get these employees to do what I wanted, when I wanted it done. I had to overhaul my way of doing things. I had to learn more about myself and my true disposition as a leader.

A personality profile instrument revealed how I was truly wired. Come to think of it, I never enjoyed the "Type A" personality approach to leading people anyway. Nurturing was more my style (my siblings were right). As I continued to grow and develop as a leader, I realized that there is no "one-size-fits-all" leadership style. All situations are different and, therefore, should be handled differently. True, successful leaders are those who can adapt their behavior to address the demands and requirements needed in their own unique situations.

The journey continues. Several opportunities presented themselves, and with each new position came new challenges. An instructor once told me about a guy who wanted to be promoted to a top executive slot. Once he got it, he stated, "They never told me that I had to lead." I don't recall thinking that, but there were times when my skill set wasn't up to par.

♥   *By this time, I had learned that good leaders recognize their deficiencies and capitalize on the strong skills of their people. You can't let your deficits get in the way.*

I respected and trusted the employees — their skill sets and their minds. We all began to soar! Once again, I had the power, but this time it was not a dirty word. It was *influence*. A leadership guru named Ken Blanchard said, "The key to successful leadership today is influence, not authority." Realizing that I had the choice to lead with authority or lead with influence, influence was a better fit for me. Understanding influence kick-started my understanding of myself.

What about the nurturing/feeling style of mine that my siblings often ribbed me about? There was more! According to them, I took too much of an interest in others' well-being. I always wanted to solve others' problems. And we cannot forget my personal favorite: "I care too much about others; that my heart is exposed! People can see it!" It took some blood, sweat and tears for me to get to the point of understanding and realize that there really is a process and method to my madness for caring about others. Experience brought with it the emergence of not only menopause but Weight, Wrinkles and yes, wonderful Wisdom. I believe there to be a direct correlation between the heart and the brain when it comes to caring for others.

The unofficial, not scientifically-studied, but real life-tested theory of why I care about others resulted in the creation of the (MCM) McIntosh Compassion Model. This phenomenon moves in a counterclockwise direction, ultimately resulting in overall emotional leadership bliss! With influence comes involvement, with involvement comes sympathy, and with sympathy comes empathy. But what is it? Believe it or not, it's a process used in my line of work just about every single day.

Most employees feel that coming to HR for any reason is comparable to visiting the "Grim Reaper." It's inevitable; but no one wants to do it. When employees finally muster up enough nerve to ask HR for help, the HR professional's initial response usually occurs with the brain, and it's quite high. The employee knows that HR should possess the *influence* (power) to help. However, the heart is not so sure it wants to help. The typical HR response is to quote company policy or procedure — perhaps even direct the employee to a state or federal law that addresses their issue or concern (*the Brain*). The employee responds with the infamous "deer in the headlight" look. It's not until the *involvement* phase that

HR begins to shift from the brain to the heart. At this point, your HR bed-side manner is on display.

In the involvement phase, you begin to lead with your heart. You are shifting into quadrant three. You are feeling. Employees will try to tell you what's bothering them, and they think they are telling you what's bothering them. But what are they really trying to tell you? The script is flipped! Now you have the "deer in the headlight" look!

Serving in HR for some 25+ years creates ninja-like skills; some would liken it to Jedi mind tricks! These skills are used to provide excellent and extraordinary service to our employees. This starts with utilizing one of the greatest tools a leader can possess: listening! Leaders mustn't just hear the employee's concern but should "discern" the employee's concerns and needs. You must listen in an active way — listen in a way that is without distraction and is absent of noise. Once involved, sympathy has kicked in; your heart begins to overtake your brain, and you begin to truly feel for the employee and their problem.

You then shift to quadrant four, where you as an HR professional are totally consumed with the issue and your brain is at its lowest point and your heart is at its highest point. It's off the charts! You now understand and feel compassion for what the employee is going through. It's important to be extra careful here, as some tend to mistake empathy for weakness. Don't fall into that trap. This is a point in the process that you must make it right. You must fix it! Those who lead from the heart know that this is GOOD!

To offer a better understanding of this phenomenon, the process is simplified via art!

McIntosh Compassion Model

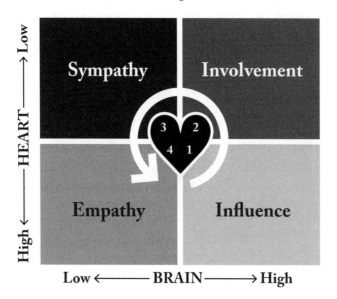

There are the four quadrants of the process: Influence, Involvement, Sympathy and Empathy — all encompassing the heart. The quadrants must be followed in sequential order — 1, 2, 3 and 4. Deviating from the process will rob you of the outcome of experiencing true compassionate bliss! Rather interesting that there are four quadrants of the Compassion model and four chambers of the human heart, isn't it?

Once the employee's issue is resolved, there is peace and understanding beyond measure; yes, compassion! It, like love, is not a noun, but a verb! It's an action that you are compelled to put legs on! Weight, wrinkles and wisdom has revealed the behavior I so graciously displayed as a young lady and was ridiculed for by my siblings has been revealed as COMPASSION! A simple, yet powerful word that simply means "to suffer together."

In a strange, yet comparative way, the same kind of ribbing I received from my siblings is often revealed in corporate America. As corporate leaders, we are tasked with both strategic and functional responsibilities of HR disciplines and competencies. Our job responsibilities may read something like this: *The Human Resources Department guides, manages and directs the overall provision of Human Resources services, policies and programs. The major areas can include: recruiting and staffing, performance management employment, compliance to regulatory concerns regarding employees, employee on-boarding, BLAH, BLAH, BLAH.* Knowing and following state and federal laws is a given for HR professionals. We got this. What I feel we don't have is the ability to truly show compassion for our employees (all while protecting the interest of the organization), and doing it in a way that is not misconstrued as "BEING WEAK." Just as my siblings criticized my caring for others, the culture of some organizations would mimic the same negative behavior.

Compassionate leadership has its own fashionable style. Some leaders, depending on how they were raised, may prefer a trench coat when it rains, whereas another may prefer a simple windbreaker. Both keep out the water; one may be a bit hotter while the other remains cool and comfortable. I challenge you to find an HR job description, specifically outlining and holding you accountable for "suffering with your employees" and that you are to take care of not only their personal needs, but those of their families. What HR job description stipulates that you be there for the employees when they are faced with adversities, catastrophic illness and, yes, even death? I am not just talking about filling out the paperwork. The compassion dive is much deeper! Truly taking on the burden of that family to the point that you cannot just sit there and do nothing, and you are compelled to act — I'm talking about that kind of compassion!

Many HR folks experience compassion every single day. There are situations we respond to with **C**aring behavior, allowing us to **O**pen our hearts and minds, providing **M**onumental support and mercy. In doing so, we **P**repare our hearts both for sadness and gladness, while we **A**dvocate for others, **S**uffering together and providing **S**ervant leadership. All the while, we **I**magine ourselves in their shoes, feeling **O**bligated to act and, ultimately, **N**urturing the human heartfelt experiences we witness by displaying kindness and empathy, HR style!

My hope is that you too are XPOSED HR Style — that you are clothed daily in Grace and Humility. Try it on! And understand that it is not "one size fits all." If it fits, it feels really GOOD! For some HR folks (and you know who you are), it feels tailor made!

"God's dream is that you and I will realize that we are family; that we are made for togetherness, for goodness and for compassion."
— Desmund Tutu —

About the Author

Dr. Milli McIntosh

Dr. Milli McIntosh currently serves as the Director of Human Resources for Simpson County Schools in Franklin, KY. She earned her Doctorate in Organizational Leadership, a Master's in Communications from Western Kentucky University and an undergraduate degree in Aviation Engineering/Technology from Southern Illinois University in Carbondale, IL. She has taught in the Communications Department at Western Kentucky University as a part-time adjunct professor.

Milli is a veteran of the U.S. Army, where she honorably served as an Officer and Helicopter Pilot.

Milli worked 20+ years in corporate America for companies, such as Brown Printing, Quebecor Printing, Tyco Adhesives, Covalence Adhesives, Berry Plastics and Georgia Pacific. She has demonstrated accomplishments in the areas of human resources, employee relations, corporate training and recruitment. Dr. McIntosh has technical knowledge and expertise in areas of Packaging and Process Engineering, Lean Manufacturing, Six-Sigma, Kaizen, 5S, Root Cause Analysis Methodology, Systems Implementation & Integration and Project Management.

She is an active member of the Mid-South Chapter of the Society of Human Resource Management (SHRM) serving as Membership Chair, and is a SHRM Senior Certified Professional. Milli also serves as an Ambassador for Franklin's Chamber of Commerce, and was recently appointed to the Executive Board of Directors for the United Way of Southern KY. She serves as a Board member for Junior Achievement, and works as needed with the Boys and Girls Club of Franklin, KY.

Dr. McIntosh, her husband Mac and their son Christjan all reside in Bowling Green, KY.

Learn more and contact Milli:
Milli.mcintosh@simpson.kyschools.us
Facebook.com/Milli.McIntosh
LinkedIn.com/in/mcintosh-resources-llc

Chapter 9

♥

Tonia Morris

"Building a Culture of Compassion, One Generation at a Time"

For some employees, a typical day at the office might begin with a barrage of work-related questions from impatient colleagues who have been awaiting their arrival. For others, it might start off with a series of cheerful greetings from co-workers, questions about how their family members are doing or perhaps an offer to grab a quick cup of coffee before the daily work deluge begins. This latter description is an ideal scenario of what a compassionate workplace would look like; it's not only more appealing, but also is vital to employee morale, teamwork and customer satisfaction.

Many leaders firmly believe that compassion has no place in the workplace. While some managers fear that showing too much kindness could be perceived as weakness, others think that pressure — not compassion — is the only way to keep employees productive.

Despite those concerns, there is actually clear evidence that compassion in the workplace serves many benefits. Compassion not only improves workplace culture, but it can also help a company's bottom line.

♥ *Cultivating a compassionate environment — one that strives to be more inclusive and increase relationships across generations — serves as a win-win situation for everyone.*

So, how would you incorporate compassion in the workplace with multiple generations having different communications style, values, work ethics and expectations?

For the first time in history, organizations are faced with how to manage a changing workforce comprised of four generations (soon to be five). Not only has the demographic of the workplace changed, but the culture has changed as well. Many ask what has changed: I would say, a lack of compassion for people of different generational backgrounds.

To build a compassionate workplace, we first must genuinely care about people regardless of age or gender; we must embrace differences and commonality. In my 20+ years working in HR, I have found that embracing the difference in others is key, and I also have found that communicating with compassion, finding ways to appreciate employees through compassion, and respecting one another will drive high retention, less-stressed employees and more engaged employees. Many organizations are faced with managing a multi-generational workplace and find it sometimes difficult to build a compassionate workplace. I believe that the workplace has changed tremendously, and it is very important to understand the four (soon to be five) generations in the workplace.

Who are the Generations in the Workplace?

I remember my days of working in Human Resources; I used to hear my colleagues stereotype the different generations, not fully understanding what value they brought to the organization. More emphasis was placed on stereotype, and less on compassion for each generation.

As HR professionals, it is vital that we incorporate compassion in every-thing we do. Human Resources along with executive management set the tone for a culture of compassion. Let's look at what has changed in today's workplace with respect to the generations.

Traditionalist is the oldest generation in the workplace. This group comprises approximately 15 percent of the workforce today, and includes everyone born before 1945.

Traditionalists respect authority and expect respect for a job well done. They are hard workers and stick to instructions given. While some of this generation may not be happy with all aspects of their jobs, they tend to follow the chain of command, don't complain, are quiet, and realize that a good paycheck means hard work. Traditionalists will usually stay with one company for most of their careers.

Baby Boomers in most organizations are the most-talked-about genera-tion. Born between 1946 and 1964, the Baby Boomer generation makes up approximately 50 percent of today's workforce. Think of this gener-ation as those who dropped out and then dropped back in. While the 1970s were fun, this group did learn to respect authority, and often hold higher management positions. They offer more ideas than Traditionalists and expect to lead, not follow.

Gen Xers, of course my generation, make up about 30 percent of the workforce and were born between 1965 and 1982. They know and under-stand technology and want to use it. Gen Xers may have many career interests and paths. They demand individuality and like multi-tasking. Gen Xers often tend to think in the "grass is greener" mode, and work/life balance is important. This generation is the independent gener-ation that embraces change, and the first generation who believed in work life balance.

The famous Millennials or Gen Y generation is admired by some and misunderstood by most. Born between 1983 and 2000, Millennials are the largest percentage of the current workforce and that percentage is on the rise every year. Boring or menial tasks are not for the Millennial worker. They not only expect technology in every form, but demand it. They would be lost without the Internet or gadgets that do everything from email, to finding directions, to deciding where to eat out at night. A dress code is not especially important to the Millennials, and they tend to seek out jobs where their creativity is most important, noticed, and rewarded.

This is the generation that is changing the way we do business, where we do business, and how we do business. Although it is the largest generation in the workplace, it is also the most misunderstood generation we've seen in decades.

Just when you thought you figured out Millennials, Generation Z is now entering the workforce. A whopping 72.8 million individuals are included in this group born between the mid-1990s and the early 2000s. We don't have a lot of data on their work expectations, but many expect it to be much different from Millennials.

Now that we have a better understanding of the different generations in the workplace, let's look at how communication has changed.

How Have Generations Changed Workplace Communication?

When you think about one of the most important soft skills needed in today's workplace, communication stands out. Communication has brought us together in many cases, and has divided us in others. We live in a society where communication is fast for some and impersonal for others.

Here's a journey about how workplace communication has changed throughout the years, as well as the most effective means of communication for employees and managers in today's workplace: The evolution of how we communicate has gone from face-to-face to typewriters, telephones, emails, conference calls, smartphones, texting and web conferencing to name a few. With a multi-generational workplace, communications have changed significantly.

Some would make the argument that we have gone from being personal to impersonal. With multiple generations in the workplace, you can be sure that you'll encounter plenty of miscommunications and misunderstandings, and less compassion, in how we communicate. As leaders, it is your job to wade through the distractions, improve verbal and non-verbal communication skills, and focus on validating the other person's experience in that moment. Validation helps to stop the fight before it begins, and takes the defensiveness out of the equation; this builds trust and a culture of compassion.

Appreciating Different Employees in Different Ways

With multiple generations now working together, it's important for organizations to take into account, when expressing appreciation to employees, that each generation has distinct characteristics.

- **Traditionalists** (1922-1945) – Want their actions to connect with the good of the company. Recognition should hone in on service and loyalty with awards, trophies and plaques.

- **Baby Boomers** (1946-1964) – Need to see how their actions make a difference. Recognition should promote and reward performance.

- **Generation X** (1965-1978) – Need flexibility to get the job done based on their schedules. Recognition should embrace these personal needs and goals.

- **Millennials** (1979-1988) – Connect their responsibilities to their personal goals. Recognition should offer tangible evidence of credibility. For example, post about the employee's career milestones on a Recognition Wall, or an internal social platform.

Something powerful occurs when we understand others from a different perspective. What seems negative can become positive. What could be considered a weakness can be viewed as a strength. What might appear as an obstacle suddenly becomes a bridge.

Can It Be as Simple as Respect?

Respect crosses generational boundaries. Talking with different generations within the workplace, we learn that respect from peers, superiors and direct reports is the top-rated workplace need of all generational groups. Conversely, expressions of lack of respect have a distinctively depressive impact on workplace productivity, creativity, and relationships.

We've all experienced it: the dismissive response, sarcastic reply, or cynical retort. Being ignored, receiving the brunt of mocking comments, rolling eyes or exclusion from conversations … sardonic remarks about age, culture, height, weight, race, gender or profession.

Taking the time to focus on others — and considering the impact of your words — goes a long way toward promoting respect. Listening without interruption and appreciating differing views communicates inclusion. Avoiding assumptions and stereotypes makes way for true understanding. When I think of respect in the workplace, I am reminded of the following quote.

"Respect appreciates the separateness of each person and recognizes their distinctive characteristics. Respect is careful to affirm people for

their intrinsic value as human beings. Respect cuts through stereo-
types and assumptions and assigns value instead of labels. "
— Cindy Saunders —

Employee Retention

One of the many benefits of compassion in the workplace is improved employee retention. After all, would you want to work for a boss who yells at you when you call in sick? Or would you prefer a boss who shows empathy for issues you experience outside the office? Creating a compassionate workplace is one of the best ways to retain employees over the long haul, which will also boost the company's bottom line.

Decreased Stress

A compassionate workplace supports employee efforts to manage stress. One simple way to reduce employee stress is to allow employees to socialize in the office. Rather than hover around the water cooler shouting at everyone to get back to work, a compassionate leader encourages employees to engage in healthy amounts of conversation.

Promoting Employee Engagement

Much has been written about employee engagement as the means to increased productivity and profitability. There is consensus on the benefits of employee engagement for employers: higher productivity, longer tenure, stronger customer relations, less healthcare usage among employees, and fewer sick days. Engaged employees reap benefits through less reported stress, higher job satisfaction, and greater satisfaction with life overall.

Engagement is one of the challenges organizations face. But, what is employee engagement? There are many definitions floating out there, but for the purpose of building a compassionate workplace, engagement is embracing all generations' uniqueness in how we communicate, and how we respect and appreciate one another.

How do you engage a multi-generational workforce? Each generational group offers valuable talents, but keeping them committed and involved is key to unlocking quality contributions. Recognizing what motivates employees is the first step to engaging them.

It's About Motivation

How can employers keep a multi-generational workforce motivated? It is not a matter of trying to get everyone to work in the same way, but about leveraging each group's strengths, and understanding what motivates them the most.

Managers shouldn't assume that they already know how to motivate employees who are older or younger. Instead, it's important to have individual conversations with workers to determine what they want out of their own professional lives.

Different Generations, Similar Expectations

While each generation has come from a different era, many suggest that in the workplace, the different generations may have more in common than employers realize, from wanting the business as a whole to succeed to wanting success in their individual careers.

When you think about building a compassionate workplace, recognize that the distinct generations have more in common than many may think. I've discovered all generations want the same things; they just approach them differently. I developed a simple solution to building a compassionate workplace: The CARE™ approach

C = Communicate

A = Appreciate

R = Respect

E = Engage

Every employee wants to be Communicated with, Appreciated, Respected and Engaged in a compassionate way at work.

Compassion is Contagious

When leaders behave in a compassionate and cooperative manner, employees are more likely to reciprocate.

Employees feel good about themselves when they're treated with compassion. As a result, they tend to want to extend those positive feelings to others. Productivity is much more likely to soar when co-workers are cooperating, rather than competing with each other's efforts.

Creating a Culture of Compassion

The good news is that any organization can introduce compassion to the workplace. A few small steps at a time can begin to make a big difference — how we communicate, cheerful greetings, conversations about family members, or simply delivering an employee a much-needed cup of coffee can set the tone for a compassionate environment. Showing people that you CARE, and creating policies that foster compassion, are simple but effective ways to improve communications, and increase retention and respect in the workplace.

About the Author

Tonia Morris, RCC

Tonia Morris, your Generational Connector,
and Founder of Tonia Morris Speaks, provides
leaders with training solutions that cultivate
a generationally-inclusive work place.

Before starting her business in 2010, Tonia was
Director of Human Resources for one of the
largest state pension agencies in the Southeast;
she has also worked in an HR leadership
capacity in other industries, including government, retail, information technology and education.

Tonia's passion for understanding the different dynamics of people led
her on a quest to solve generational issues within organizations. Tonia
noticed that the workforce was aging and changing, so she provided
training solutions on engaging and managing a multi-generational
workforce to be productive. With more than 20 years of progressive
HR experience, Tonia provides keynote speeches, lunch-and-learns, and
workshops for organizations and associations across the Southeast. She
has partnered with organizations such as Chick-fil-A, Oracle, Spelman
and Kennesaw University to name a few, to bring training solutions for
engaging Millennials in the workplace, working with leaders to transform
their cultures by attracting, developing and retaining a workforce that is
generationally inclusive.

Tonia holds a BS in Business Administration from the University
of South Florida. She currently serves on the Board of Directors
for the Millennial Chamber of Commerce, where she also

serves as the organization's HR Director, and volunteers for the Women's Entrepreneurial Opportunity Project.

She resides in Grayson, GA, with her husband of 24 years, and two sons. In her free time, Tonia loves collecting and making jewelry, and is known in the community as "the jewelry lady."

Learn more and contact Tonia:
Tonia@toniamorrisspeaks.com
www.Toniamorrisspeaks.com
LinkedIn.com/in/toniamorris

Chapter 10

♥

Stacey Oliver-Knappe

"Training Compassionate Service in a Cynical World"

It's tough out there.

It seems the world is getting to be a more difficult place to navigate. The news is full of the sad, the destructive and the criminal. Ponzi schemes and unethical businesses have taken advantage of innocent consumers. Social media allows us to be anonymous as we say hurtful things that we would never say in person to a stranger. The Great Recession has beat up many of us financially and emotionally; years later, we still feel we have not recovered.

Some days, it can feel like the worst is yet to come. It can make one pessimistic about the world, and make it seemingly impossible to do good things. We are scared and strengthening our personal defense mechanisms to deal with this unpredictability. We are becoming a world of cynics.

In her December 2012 *Psychology Today* article, Dr. Lisa Firestone writes, "Many of our cynical emotions arise when we are feeling vulnerable. In moments when we are feeling open and are let down, we are far more likely to react by toughening up and becoming defensive."

Yep, that seems to describe what I see in the workplace.

As an HR consultant, I estimate anecdotally that 80 percent of the work environments I encounter are cynical and draining, even if I have only spent a short time with the company. As a performance consultant, I am all about behaviors, and here are the behaviors I see:

- Rarely do people smile
- Leaders hide in their offices or cubicles
- Leaders only talk to employees when there is problem
- Turnover is rampant
- Communication is lacking or openly hostile
- Employees can be hostile to customers
- Metrics are emphasized more than the personal experience.

These are just to name a few.

People come to work, they grab their beverages (truly, their coping drug of choice to get them through the day), sit at their desks and get to business. There is no energy or engagement in the operation. Work environments miss warmth and a healthy dose of simply valuing and appreciating good work.

For organizations in the service industry, these environments can make providing a satisfying customer service experience all but impossible. But I have hope, and I have seen change occur, repeatedly. Change happens by focusing on compassionate customer service. It happens by moving away from the transactional focus of the business to improving the relationship between the service professional and the customer. Compassionate customer service is possible when using compassionate trainers and inventive training techniques that engage employees' hearts and minds.

Why Care About the Trainer?

In my experience, organizations focus on hanging marketing posters and giving employees tchotchkes to train their service philosophy. Sometimes, the leadership team also creates a wonderful, well-produced video stating their commitment to customer service. But if the wrong person is in the role of trainer, it can break any compassionate service initiative put forward by the organization. If your trainers don't embody the organization's service philosophy, they certainly can't teach others to deliver it successfully. This is how to ensure that the best person is in that role.

Buyer Beware of These Three Trainers

The most common path to becoming a trainer is being a high-performer in a customer service professional role. The logic goes that, if they were good at the job, then they will be good at teaching the job to others. In my experience, this is a good method to pick a trainer 60 percent of the time. The benefit is they naturally walk the talk; their heart is in it.

The challenge comes when the person is promoted, but not given the development opportunities to learn trainer skills. The person is a superstar during the demonstration portions of the training experience, and modeling is an incredibly effective training tool. The risk is that they lack the skills to transfer what they know to others. Their training mind is not fully developed.

The second common path to a training role is having tenure. These trainers simply outlasted other employees due to high turnover. Possibly, the organization is growing so rapidly that any human with longer tenure than that of a new employee is considered tenured enough to be a trainer.

This works less well for the long-term health of service organizations, but sometimes tough decisions must be made to keep the business moving forward. The benefit is that they do have some legacy knowledge, and *some* knowledge is better than none. The risk is that while they may have knowledge, were they performing best practices or using hacks to get by? Their mind is somewhat in it, but their heart could be questionable.

The final trainer — the one who causes the most damage — is the longer-tenured trainer who is burning out. How to spot this trainer? They do not welcome feedback from classroom observation. They frequently use the phrase, "That is not how we used to do it." They resist changing activities and topics in the training environment to reflect the realities of how service has evolved. They are not proactive in developing their training skills or adapting to the new technologies available to better connect to the way adults learn today.

If a burned-out trainer is not engaged with their role or the organization, the risk is that employees in training become confused and demotivated. Employees see that mediocrity is acceptable, as the leader of their learning as demonstrated. Mediocrity has no place in compassionate service.

The Compassionate Trainer

The compassionate trainer has the heart for service to all. Signs of a compassionate trainer: their technical expertise on the service provided is exceptional, and their affinity to be patient with customers shows concern for a satisfying resolution. They don't give up until a resolution is found. They work well with all members of the team, not just the ones who mirror them in skill or demeanor. They do more than is required by their job description. The best compassionate trainers are those who are genuinely nice to everyone at all organizational levels; they volunteer for a variety of projects; and they are curious. They are always asking, "What else could we do?" and eagerly seek feedback.

Once you have an effective compassionate trainer leading your service initiatives — the who — then it is time to add a bit of innovation to the training experience — the how.

Innovative Techniques

If you have been a part of a service organization, you have probably seen many different types of service philosophies being embraced. Throughout my career, I taught several different service programs that centered on acronyms. The idea is that acronyms help us to simplify and to remember a formula or actions proven to be best practices. It also gives the sense that if you do these actions, A, then customer will behave in a predetermined way, B.

I hate to break this to you, but customers are humans and fickle. It rarely happens that A + B = Happy Customer.

So, what can you do?

Innovative Technique Number 1: Use Your Name, Not Theirs

This technique is ridiculously simple. The service professional always offers their name, and more importantly, says it slowly. If it is unique, offer with it something that is memorable and humanizes them to the customer. For example, I say, "My name is Stacey, with an e," or offer a small story about why I am also called "Stacey O-K." It helps me connect.

I am shocked by how many professionals don't offer this simple compassionate action, telling customers their name. This is critical the more personal the services are. For example, in any medical situation, the professional would do a lot to show compassion toward their patient and create better patient results by sharing their name.

My mother was in the hospital for a suspected heart attack, and as one would expect, the staff came in periodically to poke and prod her. She was visibly frightened. The staff seemed to disregard her fear; not one of them offered their name to help the situation. They were doing their job, but not showing that they cared. If they had paused for a second to say, "My name is John, and I am here to take your blood pressure," it would have been a token of compassion and humanity in a scientific and scary environment.

Innovation Technique Number 2: Think Less About Acronyms and More About Accuracy

When the service professional doesn't know the policies, processes and procedures of the company, service goes badly and compassion can't even begin; consider a customer asking a question, and the service professional guessing or answering incorrectly.

One of my favorite training activities for solving this challenge involves having employees think about the top three questions or issues your customers contact you about. To get the maximum impact, these customer questions should be ones that might have upset customers due to a perceived dissatisfying resolution. It's beneficial to discuss what upsets customers the most because you can discover the compassionate answer together.

By way of example, imagine that front-desk employees are flip-charting about a common hotel check-in challenge: a guest wants to change rooms.

Once the top three challenges are defined, write each one at the top of a flip chart. If it is a class, split the class into even teams and place one team at each flip chart.

Next, have the employees write the correct answer to their question on the flip chart. Possible answers to the challenge of a guest requesting a room change are that there are no rooms available, or that the guest might want an upgrade. If it is a question that could have more than one answer, have the teams rotate among the three flipcharts to ensure that all answers make it to the chart.

To begin debriefing the activity, review all responses and check for agreement about answers. Surprisingly, my experience is that the more complicated the issue, the more likely the group doesn't agree on the answer. Yet compassionate service, by my definition, is to always provide the correct information.

To continue, discuss how employees can compassionately, kindly and sometimes firmly, deliver the correct answer to the customer. This is especially important if the customer is not going to get what they perceive they deserve. This is where the heart of the trainer can help them realize whether their answers are leaning toward ineffectual transactional phrases or effective compassionate phrases.

In our example above, the transactional response might sound like this, "We do not have any rooms for you to move to. How many room keys would you like?" Here's a compassionate answer: "I am sorry, and I know this isn't what you wanted to hear. I did my best and checked with our room assigner. The hotel is 100 percent full this evening and I won't be able to move you. How many keys would you like?"

Innovative Technique Number 3:
Forget Empathy and Go Straight to Compassion

I don't know a customer service program, except mine, that doesn't emphasize having empathy with the customer.

The formal definition of empathy, according to *Merriam-Webster's Dictionary*:

"The action of understanding, being aware of, being sensitive to, and vicariously experiencing the feelings, thoughts and experience of another of either the past or present without having the feelings, thoughts and experience fully communicated in an objectively explicit manner …"

For our context, having empathy means the service provider relates to the customer's experience and emotions; the idea is to take a walk in the customer's shoes. The problem is, it hasn't happened to the provider, so they can't walk in the customer's shoes.

Nevertheless, traditional customer service programs teach that the service professional must express empathy to move the transaction forward. Service professionals are taught to say, "I understand, but …" The problem is that it sounds condescending, and it isn't the truth. They don't understand, because they likely have not experienced this exact issue personally. It is my personal mission to remove that phrase from every service professional's lips, chats or emails, because it helps no one.

The alternative is to go straight to compassion, not empathy. Compassion is, "I get that this is rough, but I've got your back. Let me help." To get here, first develop compassion in your employees and tap into their service empowerments. My next activity helps employees see how customers need their compassion and expertise to be successful.

First, make a line on a dry erase board. On one end, draw a picture of a young child, or write the words, 1st Grader. On the other end of the line, do the same for the word Graduate.

Example

Ask the group these questions: "Based on knowledge of your company, how much do you think customers know about what they purchased or our product and service? Do they know as much as someone who just started school and has no knowledge? Do they know as much as someone who has finished school and knows all they need to know? Or are they somewhere in between?" Optional: each employee comes to the board and puts an X on their guess.

Next ask, "How would the best teacher treat a 1st grader and a graduate?" Ask, "How would they correct bad information, or tell them new information?" Expected answers: encourage them, be patient, etc.

Debrief by saying, "You are the best teacher when a customer contacts us. If you knew the customer had the same knowledge level as a first grader, how would you treat them?" Expected answers: gently, calmly, slowly, etc. Then ask, "How would you treat them if they were a graduate?" Expected answers: give them the quickest, most accurate answer. Finally, "What if they were in the middle?" Expected answers: kindly, accurately, find out what pieces the customer did not understand, etc.

End the activity by saying that they are always the best teacher during a customer contact. They are the experts and live with your organization, day in and day out. Add that they will enjoy their customers if they realize that they can educate them and quickly get them on their way, pleasantly. Just like all who teach well, if something bad or unfortunate has happened either in the customer's life or with the company, they should feel bad about it because they are another human being. Genuinely saying that they are sorry is a good thing, and helps them still to move forward with the business at hand.

In Conclusion

I have more training tips and activities, but these ideas should place you on the path to developing that dream compassionate service team. Be smart about the talent you place in the trainer role, and work consistently and diligently to develop the compassion that already exists in your workforce.

Keep a strong focus on developing compassion in your employees toward your customers so they can move beyond service transactions to service relationships.

♥ *The world can be a cynical place, but your organization can be a bright spot of compassion in your customers' complicated lives. It is your role to do your best to help your service professionals to be their best.*

About the Author

Stacey Oliver-Knappe, MA, PHR, SHRM-CP

Stacey Oliver-Knappe is the owner and chief consultant of The Customer Service Gurus, headquartered in beautiful Orlando, Florida. During her career, she has personally trained more than 10,000 people in leadership and professional development skills, and has reached many with her customized program, *The Secret to Customer Service Excellence.* Stacey has also developed training programs — rolled out to tens of thousands of employees internationally — for some of the largest companies in the hospitality industry and for customer contact centers across various industries.

Stacey's clients range from multinational corporations to small businesses and non-profits. In 2012, she started The Customer Service Gurus after devoting 15 years to developing her training expertise in corporate environments. Partnering with clients, she helps them achieve performance improvement through small actions (such as clarifying policies) and large initiatives (such as creating and implementing worldwide training programs). She is a well-praised speaker who shares her hopeful vision of customer service and human resources practices to her audiences, and a professional coach who works one-on-one with leaders.

Stacey has a master's degree in Adult Education, focusing on training and staff development, from the University of South Florida, and has earned PHR and SHRM-CP Human Resources designations. She lives in Orlando with her husband Rolf and her cats Tim and Tam, named after the amazing Australian cookie. As a devoted lifelong learner herself, she is currently working on improving her cooking skills; she has completed a marathon and is a feisty kickboxer.

Learn more and contact Stacey:
Stacey@thecustomerservicegurus.com
Website: thecustomerservicegurus.com
LinkedIn.com/in/staceyok
Twitter.com/CSGurus
Facebook.com/thecustomerservicegurus
407-495-0846

Chapter 11

♥

Jason Sackett

"Compassionate Disarming: The Key to Victory Over Anger and Grievances in the Workplace"

When a colleague or consumer unleashes a torrid, angry complaint against you — or worse, launches a formal grievance or social media campaign against your organization — you probably don't think, *This person needs a heavy dose of compassion.* Most likely, you respond with fear or anger of your own. Why should you offer compassion for someone who is being aggressive and unreasonable?

That's your ego talking. It's saying, "You're right, they're wrong, and you have moral superiority, so no need to give them anything." Although your ego wants to protect you, it can't see the big picture: a winning outcome for everyone. Would you rather be right, or win?

In times of workplace upset, to merely find relief from the conflict is not a win, and is barely a tie. True victory over confrontation means that:

- The aggrieved person feels satisfied
- Productive conversation is possible
- The complaint is resolved at the lowest level (never evolving to legal action or "public upset")

- Your relationship with this complainant has *improved*, and
- Moving forward, you never fear angry reactions or criticisms.

In the long game, winning means that your organizational culture transforms from defensive to collaborative, productivity improves, and employee retention soars. Can you imagine if you and your team had the power to create such a win? Victory is closer than you think, and compassion is the key. Here's how it works ...

Taming the Natural Responses to Confrontation

When people feel attacked, survival instincts kick in, producing one of three natural responses: *counter-attack, defensiveness,* or *submission.*

When a viral video showing aviation security officers dragging a screaming and bloody passenger from a United Express airplane subsequently provoked consumer outrage and threats of a boycott, United Airlines CEO Oscar Munoz demonstrated all three natural responses in his memos and press comments:

Counter-attack: "... this customer defied Chicago Aviation Security Officers ... He refused and became more and more disruptive and belligerent." (He blamed the victim.)

Defensiveness: "We sought volunteers and then followed our involuntary denial of boarding process ... Our employees followed established procedures for dealing with situations like this ... We remain steadfast in our commitment to make this right." (He attempted to rationalize the actions, then jumped to problem-solving.)

Submission: "The word 'shame' comes to mind ... I continue to be disturbed by what happened on this flight, and I deeply apologize." (He focused on his own feelings and repeatedly apologized.)

Do any of these satisfy you? Each natural response has serious flaws, and none mitigate the public's disgust with Munoz and United Airlines.

Defensiveness, the most common reaction to confrontation, fails to heal despite efforts to explain or resolve a situation. No matter how exquisite the justification, people are not rational when angry. They simply cannot hear explanations in that state of heightened emotion, will perceive any attempts to clarify or problem-solve as defensive, and ultimately may become more agitated.

♥ *Because natural responses can't sufficiently manage workplace conflict, we need an evolved response:* **compassionate disarming.** *This process uses absolute sincerity, listening, and empathy to thoroughly address the beliefs and feelings of the complainant, removing the energy from her grievance and diminishing her ability to direct anger toward you.*

Compassionate disarming is not a gimmick, nor is it a touchy-feely soft skill or some new form of professional cuddling. It is a highly advanced intervention designed to help you master conflict, maximize confidence for all professional interactions, and achieve total workplace victory.

Because compassionate disarming requires you to be sincere and authentic in your communications, you cannot perform it when provoked. People who attempt to disarm when they are riled or rattled come off either sarcastic (counter-attacking) or submissive; this re-arms — rather than disarms — an angry person. Therefore, a prerequisite to successful disarming is emotional self-management. Easy, right? Simply keep your cool the instant after experiencing a blindsided attack. Unless you are part android, you must capitalize on two methods for creating emotional neutrality under these circumstances: buying time, and practicing exposure therapy in advance of confrontations.

Everyone knows how to buy time, from carrying pre-planned statements for exiting conversations, to saying, "Hold that thought, I'll be back in one minute." The key is using that minute to get grounded and calm, set the ego aside, and focus exclusively on the other person before proceeding so that you are prepared to listen deeply and read the context of the situation.

Exposure therapy, also called systematic desensitization, involves deliberate immersion in artificial situations of conflict, starting with safer, easier examples. With repeated practice (exposure) in which confrontations end on a successful note, you gradually develop comfort with anger and being "attacked," until reaching the point where real-life confrontations rarely provoke you. The more sensitive a person is to anger and criticism, the more exposure he or she will need to de-condition those natural responses and react with calmness and poise.

Successful disarming also thrives off a "defusing demeanor." Despite being a slob and never doing his dishes, my college roommate was so gracious that it was hard to stay mad at him. Whenever I confronted his slovenliness, he became quiet and physically non-defensive, with open arms, palms facing upward, relaxed shoulders, and head tilted slightly forward and to the side. Had he combined this defusing demeanor with the compassionate disarming four-step technique (and washed a few more dishes), he would have held the power to win-over anyone.

Four Steps to Disarming Anger and Hostility

After establishing the foundation of sincerity, emotional management, and a defusing demeanor, you are poised to implement the compassionate disarming four-step technique:

1. Making a statement of gratitude
2. Finding truth in the complaint

3. Developing cognitive empathy

4. Demonstrating emotional empathy.

Statement of gratitude. Most compassionate disarming involves thinking on your feet to address an aggrieved person's specific needs. However, you can rehearse this step and literally carry a cheat sheet in your back pocket (see the end of this chapter for an example). Some examples include:

> *"Thank you for being so honest and direct."*

> *"I'm glad you're telling me this — it helps me."*

> *"Thank goodness someone finally said that out loud."*

> *"I wondered if people felt that way."*

How can someone offer such a response to a nasty, seemingly undeserved criticism without sounding sarcastic? Why would anyone feel sincerely grateful for incivility? Although you're entitled to resent an aggressive style and tone, whenever someone is direct, she is giving you a gift: an opportunity to listen, empathize, and repair. For that gift, you can be grateful. Passive-aggressive communication — the opposite of directness — is beyond the reach of compassionate disarming because passive-aggressive people don't admit their angry feelings and continue to deny that a problem exists; they eventually stab you in the back. Considering this, gratitude for confrontation makes sense.

Besides buying time to find truth in the complaint and build cognitive empathy, the statement of gratitude also throws complainants off balance, because no one expects a gracious reply to confrontation. An aggressive person typically anticipates a defensive or submissive response, so a statement of gratitude leaves her feeling initially confused and slightly

uncomfortable, minimizing her likelihood of feeling "rewarded" for
hostile behavior or for repeating it.

Truth in the complaint. Without exception, every complaint contains
truth — to the aggrieved person. The "truth" from your perspective is
not relevant to disarming. According to Dr. David Burns, an authority
on disarming and author of *Feeling Good Together* (2008), "Truth is the
cause of nearly all the suffering ... a battle over Truth nearly always fuels
the hostilities." The key to this step is identifying the other's truth, and
agreeing with the elements that you can sincerely acknowledge. After
United's debacle, Oscar Munoz had a golden opportunity to narrate the
truth in the complaint, because the video clearly portrayed it:

> *"This video shows United Representatives forcibly removing a terrified
> passenger from one of our planes, injuring him in the process. This
> behavior appears aggressive, unprofessional, hurtful, and humiliating to
> the passenger, and disturbing to everyone."*

Had Mr. Munoz said this, he would have begun steering the conversation
away from the firestorm of public upset, instead of making it worse with
defensiveness. Notice that finding truth in this complaint *does not increase
liability*, because it involves acknowledging only what is plainly visible or
unequivocal. If you find this hard to believe, read the example from my
bio about my dog Cupcake who bit a personal injury lawyer!

In some complaints, the truth is less obvious. Following a workshop
that I had considered to be one of my best, a participant approached
me and said, "You are bar none the worst facilitator I have ever had to
tolerate." Yes, this really happened. What's the truth in this complaint?
Because I don't agree with this person's conclusion, I can't honestly say,
"You're right, I'm incompetent." However, after a quick statement of
gratitude, and without compromising sincerity, I can say, "Clearly, what

I delivered today did not work for you." That's enough truth to carry me to the next step.

Cognitive empathy. Most of your compassionate disarming effort will encompass developing cognitive empathy. Often, with only a few words from the complainant, you must thoroughly and accurately understand his perspective, including why he considers the issue important, and how his needs and expectations are not being met. Then, you communicate that understanding, while continuing to resist explaining or defending your actions.

After acknowledging the truth in the complaint against United Airlines, Oscar Munoz could have taken advantage of the video's detail to offer a thorough, compassionate identification of issues:

> *"When people fly, they often feel stressed, tired and eager to reach their destinations. They want to feel cared for, relaxed and safe, and they expect airline personnel to treat them with professionalism, dignity and respect. The behavior of our representatives on this flight fell far below these expectations, and has left our customers feeling disrespected, unappreciated and more stressed. No one ever wants to see a passenger man-handled, much less injured."*

In the case of my workshop critic, I have only 13 words to work with: "You are bar none the worst facilitator I have ever had to tolerate." Still, after resisting a sarcastic comeback, conjuring some compassion, and completing the first two steps, I can develop considerable empathy from the context, highlighting what matters to him and why:

> *"When you came to this workshop, you invested valuable time to learn needed skills, and you trusted me to help you acquire those and provide you with a positive experience. At this point, you can't get back your time; you had a dissatisfying experience; and you still need the skills."*

Did I leave out anything? I have addressed all the issues I can glean from this context, and he is about 80 percent disarmed. For total victory, I need one more step.

Emotional empathy. After successfully performing steps one to three, demonstrating emotional empathy is a breeze, requiring only a sincere acknowledgment of the complainant's feelings:

> (What Oscar Munoz could have said to the public): "Everyone, especially the people that experienced this behavior first-hand, would rightfully feel angry about that treatment and outraged with United. I am sorry that this happened and for the impact these actions caused."

> (Me, to Angry Workshop Guy): "I can see how you would feel angry about that lost time and lack of skill acquisition, and I'm sorry you had to endure that."

What would happen if you tried to lead with emotional empathy, identifying the complainant's anger from the start? Without first demonstrating understanding of her perspective and truth in the complaint, you haven't yet earned the right to name her anger. Therefore, she would most likely spit back your compassion with, "Don't tell me how I feel!"

Exploring a complaint before demonstrating emotional empathy can also be risky, as it may inadvertently invite more attacks. If I asked Workshop Critic, "Can you tell me what parts didn't work for you?," how might he respond?

> "Everything!"

> "Only every word you said, until 'the end.'"

> "If you don't know, then you're even dumber than I thought."

After concluding emotional empathy, it's wise to check in with the complainant (for example, "Did I miss anything?") to evaluate how disarmed she is, confirm that you addressed all issues, and ask questions to explore any loose ends. If successful, you are ready to move to problem-solving or a broader conversation.

Avoiding Re-Arming

When attempting compassionate disarming, the least desirable outcome is "re-arming" the aggrieved person. I have already demonstrated how explaining, problem solving, speaking when provoked or without sincerity, and clinging to being right will undermine efforts and escalate your critic. Besides avoiding these, it is crucial to remove from your vocabulary the three "deadly sins" of disarming:

"I understand."

"I know how you feel."

"I'm sorry if..."

Uttering any of these will compel the complainant to respond:

"No, you DON'T understand!"

"No, you DON'T know how I feel!" (possibly preceded by nasty expletives)

"IF?!"

What About Apologizing?

Apologies are less powerful than compassionate disarming because to offer one does not require any true understanding or empathy for another's feelings. However, because social convention influences many people to expect an apology, it is helpful to include one following emotional empathy. One sincere "I'm sorry" prevents the tragic outcome of executing the perfect disarm, followed by the complainant saying, "Well, I still haven't heard you apologize," nullifying all your hard work. Limiting yourself to one apology, you satisfy the social expectation, but avoid appearing submissive with multiple apologies that often embolden and re-arm a complainant.

Practice, and Win

If you can master the art of compassionate disarming, you will have it all: confidence and freedom from fear in all exchanges, enhanced professional relationships, a healthier corporate culture and public image, a more stable and productive work force, a more loyal consumer base, and a dramatic reduction in grievances and legal action. I wish this chapter alone could get you there, but you and your colleagues will need regular exposure to increasingly challenging confrontations to become consistently masterful, compassionate disarmers.

Fortunately, once you have absorbed the concepts, you can create ample practice opportunities provided you have a partner willing to criticize you. Colleagues and friends are fine, but significant others are the ultimate test. Because they know you well, and the stakes are high in romantic relationships, they are among the most difficult people to disarm. (No matter what, don't tell yours that you read this chapter!). Succeed with him or her, and you're ready to disarm in the business world. Resist natural responses, find compassion for the aggrieved — regardless of how unreasonable they may seem — and you will win.

Compassionate Disarming Pocket Guide

Be sincere. Ground yourself. Use a defusing demeanor.

1. **Make a statement of gratitude.**
   ("It helps me that you told me that.")

2. **Find truth in the complaint.**
   ("Yes, that happened.")

3. **Develop cognitive empathy.**
   ("___ didn't meet your needs/expectations.")

4. **Demonstrate emotional empathy.**
   ("I can see ___ made you angry. I'm sorry.")

Evaluate your effectiveness. ("Did I miss anything?")

www.ManagingUpset.com

About the Author

Jason Sackett, PCC, LCSW, CEAP

Jason Sackett helps organizations become compassionate masters of
conflict, providing compassionate disarming training, keynote speaking,
and train-the-trainer programs. He also offers public upset executive
coaching through which CEOs and other public figures genuinely transform from villain to hero.

He has recorded many victories over conflict, but none greater than the
time his dog, Cupcake, bit and injured a personal injury lawyer, who

never pursued litigation after experiencing Jason's compassionate disarming technique in action. His success comes from expert training, constant practice, and 25 years of professional experience dealing with aggrieved, hostile, and fundamentally unreasonable individuals — and the unlucky people who work with them.

Jason has trained hundreds of professionals in compassionate disarming, has coached business owners and C-suite executives with volatile teams and ornery consumers, and has facilitated more than 350 workshops. He has taught graduate-level courses in forensic social work, and published dozens of articles and training video clips to help people overcome conflict and win at work.

Jason holds a Master of Industrial Social Work from the University of Southern California, and received a BA in Anthropology from the University of California, Berkeley. He is credentialed by the International Coach Federation (ICF) as a Professional Certified Coach (PCC), is a Licensed Clinical Social Worker in California, and holds a Certified Employee Assistance Professional (CEAP) credential. Jason is also trained and certified as an Executive Coach Supervisor.

Learn more and contact Jason:
Jason@SolutionsMine.com
310-251-2885
ManagingUpset.com and SolutionsMine.com
LinkedIn.com/in/jasonsackettlcsw
Twitter.com/jasonsackett

Chapter 12

♥

Dr. Amy M. Smith

"Ignite Compassion: Create a Corporation with Heart"

Today, I walked into chemo. That's significant because I walked into chemo. During the past year, I have struggled in, hobbled in, held an arm to be supported in. I'm in treatment for breast cancer. Nowhere is compassion as much a part of the workplace as in a cancer infusion center. I have a group of 10 amazing people at my infusion center and six at my radiation clinic who are the pure embodiment of compassion in the workplace.

What you see in a cancer clinic is tremendous suffering. A 20-something newlywed with brain cancer, suffering through painful chemo that takes more than six hours to deliver. A grandmother who curls up in her chair, resembling a child in the womb, to combat the stomach and muscle spasms that are a side effect of her treatment. A mom of two high-school-aged boys with radiation burns so severe that she must postpone her treatment.

There's a bell in our clinic. You ring it when you finish a round of treatment or, better, complete your treatment. Yet, everyone hesitates. They don't want to make those who are still fighting feel bad about where they are in their journey. Once muscled into ringing the bell, each patient receives a chorus of applause from all who hear it — in the halls, the lab, the offices and from the infusion chairs. Every time. Those who suffer together, rejoice together.

What you also see in a cancer clinic is tremendous compassion. Patients help the newly diagnosed pick out a wig, manage side effects with home remedies and support one another when treatments become unbearable. My oncologists, my nurse practitioner, my infusion and oncology nurses, my radiation technicians, my friends who run the offices — all of these people — demonstrate compassion on a daily basis. If you are diagnosed with something unimaginable and find yourself with a team that doesn't show compassion in every interaction, fire them. Find another one. In this type of workplace, compassion is a commodity that makes or breaks a business. My cancer team? Well, they're a beautiful model of how a workplace should be.

What a Difference a Little Perspective Can Make

Before I was diagnosed, I was "a lost ball in the tall grass," as my daddy would say. That's a Kentucky analogy for being clueless. In our workplace, a financial institution, we were all clueless. It was late winter and time for our executive management team to review employee handbook policy. As my peers and I discussed Family Medical Leave Act (FMLA) allotments, I watched as the discussion polarized the group. Two of my peers were adamant that 12 weeks of FMLA leave were not enough. They argued that three months to an employee dealing with a serious illness wasn't nearly compassionate enough. Couldn't we extend FMLA leave another month or make a determination based on individual employees?

I understood. In the past 20 years, we'd had employees work until their illnesses took their toll and they passed away. We had employees with illnesses that stole critical thinking skills and impacted their ability to work. We had a few employees with a terminal diagnosis, but they continued to rebound and work productively, even after extended absences. These were employees we cared for and valued, and who worked hard and productively.

Across the table, another peer referred to the policy, fairness in treating all employees equitably and the need for business to continue in an employee's absence. How could we financially carry employees when they could not work? How could anyone leave a job open for three months and still meet goals? How is it fair to the employees who cover the other employee's work? Twelve weeks should be the firm limit.

I understood this, too. Our organization had battled back from the impact of the recession like so many other companies. We had gone through downsizings and rightsizings and reorganizations. While financially stable, we certainly weren't at the point where compassion for employees could comfortably outweigh the financial need to have key jobs filled.

As our human resources director began giving examples of how we had handled cases of previous employees who had exhausted their FMLA, my mind whirled with questions. How can we be both an organization that acts with compassion toward an employee and also one that upholds high standards of accountability? How can I ensure we have fair, accountable human resource policies that have wiggle room for individual employee circumstances? One thing was clear: None of us had ever had a serious illness, so none of us could make this decision from personal experience.

Fast-forward six months. My annual mammogram revealed a mass — breast cancer. Immediately, I missed six weeks of work, as surgery, tests and a second, smaller surgery and recovery took place. My husband and I had almost frantic conversations about how I would continue to work, when the treatment plan called for 18 months of chemotherapy and 35 days of radiation. How would we continue to pay bills that took two salaries to support? How could we pay new medical bills that added up quickly, causing a financial burden? If I couldn't return to work, how would we be able to pay the $75,000 weekly chemo treatment without health insurance?

As I counted every FMLA hour charged to my dwindling account of medical leave, I wondered how my organization would view my absence. Was I missed enough for them to know I was an important part of the team? Was I missed so much that management would feel the need to fill my position before I was well enough to return? Policy needed to be flexible enough to give people faith that their employer would help them remain a contributing part of the organization. Yet, policy needed to be strong enough to support business needs. So, how do you become an organization that leads its business strategy with compassion?

Balance Accountability with Grace

As humans, we have enormous potential to show compassion. It's the way God wired us. However, things get in our way — our own needs, needs of our immediate families, the busyness of life, even being a little clueless to the suffering of those around us. We may all be, from time to time, lost in the tall grass.

Mia's Story: Consider Mia, an employee with great potential, a strong work ethic and a mind that always looked to solve problems. Taking on her first big assignment, she got in a little over her head and her pride wouldn't let her ask for help. Unfortunately, the results were public and hard to recover from, so Mia resigned. Policy stated that resignations were accepted, unless a request was made from the employee and approved by the executive director to rescind the resignation. Balancing accountability with grace, Mia's supervisor made a case for a verbal reprimand and a request for the employee to remain in her position, which was approved. A year later, the organization had a loyal employee who, through coaching and collaboration, was an example of accountability and grace in an organization.

Lincoln's Story: Leave of absence policy often pushes employees into an "us-versus-them" scenario, especially when FMLA comes into play. Lincoln was no different: for 10 of his 12 weeks of FMLA, he avoided Human Resources despite our attempts to offer him assistance or update him on how much FMLA leave he had remaining. What would happen when his FMLA coverage was over? His illness was terminal, but to Lincoln, work was important. Work gave him snatches of time when he didn't think about being sick. What he had contributed for 15 years to the company was a kind of legacy.

When Lincoln neared the end of his FMLA period, the organization had a pivotal choice to make: follow policy or explore how policy could meet both the organization's needs and the employee's needs? What was best for the organization and the employee would be for Lincoln to transfer his organizational knowledge to other key staff. After conversations with Lincoln, the supervisor created opportunities for Lincoln to work both remotely and in the office to train two key staff on his work. When the time came for Lincoln to transition away from work, staff were prepared to handle his absence, and he felt good about the work legacy he was leaving behind.

♥   *Corporations can manage accountability with grace when they take a moment to consider what is in the best interest of the organization and the employee. Recognizing the human condition — that we all suffer — is the first step.*

Second, ask how policy can be used to do what is best for the organization. Finally, determine if there is a way to also meet needs of valuable employees by learning their stories. When you put a name, a face, a story to suffering, it changes everything.

Hire Employees with Heart

Organizations can ignite employee-generated compassion; simply hire employees with a heart, and they will lead and serve with compassion. I work for a financial institution. Employees with finance backgrounds are not often seen as having a heart for more than business needs. I have had the privilege to work with some of the most compassionate, financially-minded business people anywhere. We hire them because they have that rare combination of a missional heart and a sound business mind. It's a combination that works.

Sophie's Story: When their company lost its executive director and a portion of its management team through a reorganization, Josh, Sophie and Chuck were uncertain about the future. They felt like most other employees —scared, uncertain, a little angry. Sophie proposed a lunch-hour prayer group to the Human Resources team but, due to policy, the director recommended they meet off-site and not use corporate resources. With a heart to help employees, but no power within the organization, the employees held a lunch meeting off campus. When gathered, they spoke aloud the names of employees who had been laid off, and prayed for their mental and financial health and their job searches. The group spoke the names of the leaders who were gone and those still running the organization. They prayed for guidance for them, and prayed for the new leader — yet to be chosen. Finally, they prayed for the health of the organization.

An Organization's Story: During the heart of the recession, our Human Resources team learned staff were struggling. The price of peanut butter increased. A can of spaghetti sauce was still $1.00, but it was 8 oz.

smaller, which meant a family had to buy two for the same pre-recession meal. Gas prices were on the rise. On the corporate side, the organization had announced furloughs, and line-level employees struggled to meet their financial obligations. Most disheartening, we were hearing stories from employees who were unable to buy school supplies or Christmas gifts. Human Resources staff took up cash donations and discreetly shared them.

Soon, to manage this fairly, management felt policy and structure was needed. After a lengthy discussion, the organization decided staff should not collect money and transfer it to employees. The cash would be considered "pay" subject to taxes and normal withholding, lessening the amount given to the employee, and causing it to falsely inflate their salary on record. Not to be swayed, staff cleaned out an office and, leaving it unlocked, encouraged employees to leave groceries and take groceries — no questions asked. We offered financial planning and couponing lunch-and-learns. When Christmas came, donations that had normally gone to a local charity were re-directed to fill stockings of staff's children and gifts from employees to employees, quietly shared through our Human Resources office.

How do you find employees with heart? They can be found during the interview. Add a compassion question into your interview process:

- Tell me about a time when you used compassion to address a workplace challenge.

- Give me an example of a time when you helped a coworker whose work was suffering.

- How can you tell when a coworker needs help? Tell me about a time you have helped someone without being asked.

- Tell me about a time when you had to deliver difficult news.

When an organization hires employees with heart, in conjunction with — or in spite of — policy, a workplace benefits from compassion. When you hire the right people and they see suffering, compassionate ideas follow.

Balance Business Needs with Compassion

In the past 10 years, organizations have used techniques such as work furloughs, downsizings, reorganizations and rightsizings to meet business needs. We've all heard stories of employees who learned they were laid off from a news story or from a letter. Impersonal, but practical, this type of human resource practice is an easy way to deal with a business need. How much more time and effort, even money, would it take to end a mutually beneficial relationship with a little compassion?

Like many other organizations, my workplace has been through furloughs, downsizings, rightsizings and reorganizations since 2009. During a closure of two offices, we let people know immediately, with a message that outlined business needs, but also honored the contributions employees had made. We had human resources staff ready to speak privately with the employees and offered help with resumes. We provided a severance package and gave employees several months' notice with paid time away from work to interview. We connected employees to a program that helped pay mortgages after a job loss. As hard as those times were for our employees, we had people thank us for the way we downsized. I'm always humbled and amazed when that happens.

If you're wondering how my FMLA story turned out, it has a good ending. Our organization has an FMLA policy that balances fairness with ensuring continued business operations. The employee handbook leaves post-FMLA policy open to allow performing staff to work remotely, make up hours and preserve their leave time, and work reduced schedules. This saves in turnover and recruiting costs, and gives a performing employee who can return to work a bridge to extend their time. We treat employees who cannot return to work and their caregivers with compassion by offering legal services, providing support to complete insurance paperwork and ensuring benefits coverage continues for as long as possible. Through this compassionate policy, our corporation has been able to retain several high-performing employees who have battled terminal illnesses and worked until either hospice care was needed or they were no longer capable. What better way to offer compassion than to help a valued employee feel good about their work legacy, ensure their family receives designated benefits, and ease some of the financial burdens of final care plans?

Business decisions and compassion for employees don't have to be mutually exclusive. If your organization, you and your coworkers have a heart that cares for people, your business decisions will follow and compassion ignites. This past year has been challenging for me, both personally and as an employee. I'm no longer lost in the tall grass — I understand what it means to receive compassion in the workplace. As an employee, I don't want to work somewhere where policy and compassion can't find a home together. Even when we have just a little to give, there is someone to whom our "little" means the world.

About the Author

Amy M. Smith, PhD

Dr. Amy M. Smith supports strategic organizational development and employee engagement through her role as Deputy Executive Director with Kentucky Housing Corporation, the state's housing finance agency, where she has been employed for more than 23 years. With a doctorate in human resource development, Amy works to develop a workplace environment that has the right conditions for all members of the organization to give their best each day. By encouraging employees to understand and commit to their company's strategic goals, Amy hopes to create a legacy of employees who are motivated to contribute to organizational success, and who have an enhanced sense of their own value in the workplace.

Amy is a graduate of Georgetown College, with a degree in English and American Studies, and of the University of Louisville, where she received an MA in English and a PhD in Human Resource Development, with an emphasis in organizational development.

Amy lives in Frankfort, Kentucky, with her husband, Scott; her three children, Hannah, Ben and Sophie; and her spoiled ninja kitten, Mango. Her greatest joy comes from her relationships with those around her, including her family, friends and coworkers. In her free time, she enjoys baking, crafting and hanging out with her kiddos.

Learn more and contact Amy:
Asmith1739@gmail.com
Twitter.com/asmith1739_amy
LinkedIn.com/in/dr-amy-smith-phd-a75a064

Chapter 13

♥

Ben St. Clair

"Compassion@Work – Doing Well by Doing Good"

"It was devastating. Hurricane Katrina hit my hometown, New Orleans. My family's home was destroyed, and so was my mom's. We were so scared and shaken. We evacuated to northern Louisiana for a period as the storm and its aftermath played out.

My company, the one I'd joined just two weeks earlier in a sales role to serve the New Orleans area, tracked me down to make sure I was okay. They made a deposit in my bank account to help my family get through the near term. They kept me on the payroll even though I couldn't work in our community for months.

That happened over ten years ago. I'm still here. I'm proud to be part of a compassionate, caring organization that thinks beyond the bottom-line, one that genuinely cares about its associates. I'm staying as long as my company will have me. Every day I try to show the same compassion and humanness to the people I serve in my role as a manager."

— Rebecca R.

Let's hope that no one we know is ever in a situation like Rebecca's. What a blessing that she works for a compassionate organization.

Somewhere in her company's history, leaders consciously decided that they stood for doing the right thing, by caring about people and responding to challenging situations in a compassionate way. They consciously decided to be that kind of company.

Companies do well by doing good. Rebecca's company experienced the self-satisfaction of their humanitarian response. They've continued to benefit, too, from Rebecca's company advocacy, associate engagement, loyalty, long-term tenure, and culture-aligned leadership behaviors.

Compassion literally means to suffer together. A compassionate response is one that facilitates assistance to help the sufferer. Rebecca's company demonstrated a compassionate response to her difficult, life-changing situation. They identified her suffering, acknowledged it, and conveyed a desire to alleviate or reduce it. It was an exemplary compassionate response.

Compassion is an emerging business topic; new publications appear almost daily. Two dimensions of compassion at work are being addressed in the literature. The first focuses on why and how to cultivate a more compassionate workplace and organizational culture. The second dimension is externally focused. Much is being written about companies that are enlisting compassion as a core business strategy. These companies seek to solve social problems, and to do so in ways that improve their bottom lines.

Compassion as a Personal Competency

Compassion is a way to make workplaces more human. A compassionate workplace invites people to bring their entire selves to work, setting the stage for higher productivity and innovation. Through compassion, we acknowledge those for whom life, or a moment, is a struggle. We convey to them a sincere attitude of caring, and the desire to help and to relieve their struggles. The gesture may enable them to feel safe, find more peace, and to be better employees. Those employees then bring a higher percentage of their whole and best selves into their tasks, their interactions with colleagues and customers, and their homes and communities.

Compassion isn't easy for all leaders. Leaders may worry that it could mark them as "soft" or as someone who wastes time and resources on matters not directly linked to key business metrics. Or, for some, it just goes against the grain; they may have been taught that pressure, not compassion or other humanistic tactics, is the way to keep people productive.

Compassion impacts the bottom line. The University of Michigan's Ross School of Business has studied compassion in the workplace. Their research shows that, instead of hurting productivity, compassion at work improves associate engagement, retention, customer ratings and profits. The University of California at Berkeley has found that identifying and attempting to relieve suffering in the workplace increases employee satisfaction and loyalty, reduces stress and related illness, fosters positive work relationships, increases cooperation, and improves customer relations.

Let's go from abstract to real: This true story illustrates a compassionate response to a workplace situation. Notice the situation and then the behaviors that form the compassionate response.

> *I was walking into our office building. Sis called, crying. Mom had passed. We talked. I continued into the office, trying to be stoic but feeling a little lost and in shock. Two work friends, Shonna and Deborah, must have noticed or I mumbled something. They checked on me. We went for coffee. We sat together. I shared the news, and a few tears. One sat next to me; the other moved to my other side. I felt so comforted by their kindness, their humanness, and their gentle, thoughtful comments. They listened. I don't recall what I said, or what they said. What I remember is that*

they were with me in a moment of suffering. And their gesture made it better. I found my center again and continued into the days and weeks that followed. Years later, I still value and care about these two kinds people. I appreciate what they did for me. They also taught me about compassion, and how to be there for someone. I'm proud and lucky to work in a company where that human and humane spirit is present.

— Olin B.

What made this an effective response? Olin's co-workers know and care about each other enough to notice when someone is having an off moment. When they saw cues, they responded. They didn't ignore Olin's nonverbal signals. They didn't shut him down or send him home. They identified Olin's situation (or suffering), approached, inquired, and responded with a sincere desire to alleviate or reduce his suffering. They didn't attempt to solve his problem or take it away. Their response made a positive difference for Olin and for his work team and organization. If situations like this make you or others feel awkward or ill-equipped, remember Olin's story and the way his colleagues responded. It's a textbook example of compassion done well.

"Be kind. Everyone you meet is carrying a heavy burden."
— Ian McLaren —

Here's another example. It illustrates the same response model. It works. Plus, notice that there are people all around us carrying heavy burdens. We may help them or even change their lives by noticing and responding compassionately.

I wanted to tell my mother that I'm gay. I was scared about her potential reaction. Yet, I was at a crossroad. I needed to tell her. No more secrets. I was distraught and emotional. A colleague noticed my suffering. We talked. That led to the idea that I should approach one of our managers, one who reminded me of my mom — similar age and background. I met with her. I couldn't help myself — I poured my heart out. The manager responded in an accepting, compassionate way. She even helped me rehearse the conversation with my mom. The interaction changed everything. I went on to have the conversation with my mom. It was a loving, accepting conversation that made our lives better. The co-worker who noticed my suffering and engaged me, the manager who responded compassionately and helped me — they changed my life. Our connection will last a lifetime, as will my positive association with the company that I've grown to think of as my work home.

— Kathleen H.

What to do when really bad things happen? Sometimes bad things happen to our colleagues or their loves ones. We don't know what to do. Here's a piece of guidance that has helped others.

When something bad happens, if there's a tragedy for a friend or loved one like a challenging health situation, an accident or the death of a loved one, I've learned that it's not about me or about what I'm feeling. What I need to do is show up and be of service. Maybe it's texting with them, calling them, bringing coffee, greeting and hugging people, tidying up, smiling, making a store-run for the forgotten item, or something else. What I can bring to difficult, emotional situations is my presence, my physical or virtual self and singleness of purpose to be of service. I don't have to know the perfect thing to say or do. In fact, the less I say, the better. I'm not there to solve the problem. I just have to be present; focus on the needs of others rather than my feelings; and do the next right thing, that I have faith will be revealed to me.

— Kati E.

Social media is a game-changer for compassion. Facebook, Twitter, SnapChat, Instagram and other apps make it easier and faster than ever for people to support each other in good times and bad. Social media can help leaders rapidly expand the expression of compassion in the workplace.

> *I knew that our internal social media platform was more than a communication platform, and that it was an actual community, early in Buzz's existence when one young father posted about the loss of his precious daughter who only lived for a few days. The grieving father was open and bold enough to share beautiful photos of him holding his daughter, and he told the heart-wrenching story of her passing. Associates showed up in droves through comments, emails and phone calls — many of them in tears — as they grieved with him. People who chose not to respond online contacted me in a variety of ways to tell how the story impacted them. I asked the father for permission to feature his story alone in that week's summary broadcast, and the outpouring of compassion resulting from that exposure remains a milestone in the platform's history. We are a true community of people who care about one another.*

— Jeff R.

Celebrating joy is also part of compassion. An emerging concept in compassion research is called co-passion. Researchers propose that sharing in the positive emotions and joy of others provides personal and organizational benefits. Remember how you felt the last time an individual or group authentically joined you in your moment of joy? Maybe it was a remark, beaming smile, social media post, high-five or impromptu celebration. For many people, such a response amplifies and prolongs the good feeling. It improves the human spirit in the workplace that the University of Michigan and Cal Berkeley have shown enhances engagement, productivity, customer ratings and profitability.

*"If you want other people to be happier, then practice compassion.
If you want to be happier, then practice compassion."*

— 14th Dalai Lama —

Compassion – As a Business Strategy

Compassion can be a business strategy. More companies are recognizing that doing good in the world around them ultimately improves their bottom line. In fact, *Fortune* now annually publishes a list of companies that include in their mission the desire to change the world.

Fortune says the companies on the list seek to solve social problems and to do so in ways that improve their bottom line. It's a core business strategy for them rather than something they do through their philanthropic entity. These companies believe there is a stakeholder beyond the shareholder, and they don't see it as a tradeoff. They are embracing a new leadership paradigm.

Humana Inc., my employer, is a company that takes this approach. Humana provides health coverage and related well-being products and services for people throughout the United States. The company has transformed its organization in recent years through a strategic commitment to positive social change.

It's been interesting and educational to observe the company's journey and transformation. Here are some things Humana has done to deploy compassion as a business strategy.

Bold Goal. An important part of pursuing compassion as a business strategy is having an enterprise-wide agreement on strategic intent. One way to do this is to document, publish and champion the intention. Humana is in the health and well-being business. Company executives agreed on a compassion-based strategic intent and put it in writing. Here is what Humana leaders wrote:

> *Our Bold Goal is to help make the communities we serve 20 percent healthier by 2020 by making it easy for people to achieve their best health. Through physician, non-profit, business and government partnerships we are dedicated to finding solutions to complex health problems. Together, we are addressing social determinants of health like food, insecurity, loneliness and social isolation because good health is good for everyone. Join us!*

It will require hard work and change. For many companies, shifting to a dual focus on changing the world and meeting bottom line targets is a transformational change. Here are a few of my observations of things Humana has done to broaden its focus.

Build Out. Transforming a company's business model means change. Humana revisited and updated its company values to reflect its dual focus on positive social change that improves the bottom line. Three of five company values have a humanistic intention: cultivate uniqueness, thrive together, and inspire health. The final two, rethink routine and pioneer simplicity, guide the organization in getting there. The company has also adjusted its metrics and reporting, organizational design, communication strategies, staffing and more. For example, in addition to its traditional financial annual report, the company also publishes reports of comparable depth and quality on social change initiatives, including an Inclusion & Diversity Report and a Corporate Social Responsibility Report.

Force for Good. Enlisting associates is critical. Everyone must feel and have alignment to the compassion business strategy. That's not easy, but the journey there is where the value resides. Humana does many things in this regard. Associates have a paid volunteer day per year. Leaders encourage associates to use the time, and often invite colleagues into additional community activities aligned to inspiring health. Associates are encouraged to be vigilant for opportunities to support or participate in health-related events in the communities we serve. Stories of good works are often shared throughout the company. Everyone can share in the joy and positivity associated with our bold goal and pursuit of it. We have an incredibly positive and compassionate organizational culture.

> *"If companies become a force for good, the people working for them will be that much more motivated and their brands will shine that much brighter amongst others."*
>
> — **Sir Richard Branson** —

Doing Well by Doing Good

♥ *Compassion makes a difference in the workplace, yet it's not an innate competency for everyone. Leaders have a role in cultivating a compassionate workplace through their authentic responses to both the suffering and joy of others.*

There is a compassionate response model that can guide anyone in learning to respond effectively in situations where a response will make a difference. Employee stories make it clear that compassion at work improves their lives. Business researchers back it up with science, showing that compassion can improve associate engagement, retention, customer ratings and profits.

Compassion can be taken to another level by embracing it as a business strategy. It's becoming more common for companies to pursue the dual focus of social change that impacts the bottom line as well as traditional capitalistic intentions. They choose to aspire to change the world and do well by doing good. There are leading academic institutions doing research on the topic to help advance the cause and there are organizations, like Humana, that are well down the path in their journey and have insights and lessons to share. Compassion as a business strategy — doing well by doing good — may offer a new, invigorating, and profitable opportunity for many organizations.

"Compassion is the radicalism of our time."

— The 14th Dalai Lama —

About the Author

Ben St. Clair

Ben St. Clair helps companies improve human and organizational performance. He is a Learning Consultant for Humana Inc., a company that provides health and well-being solutions, where he designs and implements human performance solutions that support the rollout of new business strategies, and resolve existing performance challenges. Ben enjoys being part of a company that has compassion as part of its culture and business strategy, and is grateful for Humana and his "work family."

Ben has more than 20 years' experience in both internal and external consulting roles in learning and development, and performance improvement. He earned a BA in Psychology from Washington & Lee University, an MA in Psychology from the University of West Florida, and an MS in Business Communication & Leadership from Spalding University.

If you're interested in compassion at work, performance improvement, learning and development, leadership development or similar topics — or you just need a little compassion today — connect with Ben.

Learn more and contact Ben:
dgtben@gmail.com
LinkedIn.com/in/ben-st-clair-9252235

Chapter 14

♥

Carole Stizza

"Compassionate Curiosity: The 5-lb Workout with the 100-lb Result"

The moment I realized how profound curiosity is when it comes to engaging one another in meaningful conversations, I was working with a new client. He seemed to have his mind made up on almost every topic I brought forth and was blind to those affected. I then asked, "What are you curious about?" The entire conversation shifted, and as I continued to ask questions, there was a monumental shift in what he wanted to achieve *and* he suddenly found his compassion for how decisions affected those around him.

Applying this curiosity theory repeatedly since then has impacted my entire outlook on interacting with clients, coworkers and family in helping them shift profoundly. Granted, curiosity is not a new concept.

♥ *But as a society, we have used "curiosity" less than any other generation before us — we have, in a sense, become less curious. We're not less curious about stuff that doesn't matter, but about people who do matter.*

I now use curiosity to drive more compassionate conversations for the following effects. Curiosity can:

- Diffuse drama
- Increase accountability
- Drive innovative results, and
- Nurture richer conversations.

How does *THAT* work?

Think about when you were curious about solving a problem. Did you stop and get flustered about how you felt, or were you so focused on learning that you were more open-minded to what showed up?

I'm not referencing the "next shiny object" curiosity here. I'm referencing "empathic" curiosity, the ardent desire to know about others. This type of curiosity has been found to bypass the ego, open the mind to being more receptive to information and ideas, and create a connection between you and whoever is in the path of your curiosity.

Face it, when we are curious about someone else, we ask questions. By asking questions, we help the recipient feel valued. By listening to the person's answers, additional details emerge for you; but more importantly, your listening re-humanizes the other with caring and empathy. Empathy evolves from having enough information to understand the other's point of view. You don't have to agree with it — let's be clear — we are all different for a reason. But, we do need to know how others think. This introduces compassion, the ability to understand someone else's suffering. This is a large idea to heed.

Compassion at work is about understanding how decisions made at work affect where, why or how people may suffer because of those decisions. When we are talking about bringing compassion into the workplace, and we need to know where to apply it, how it will be received, and who will be affected by it the most, we would do well to start with curiosity. Being curious starts a process that gets us to compassion faster than you may realize. More importantly, curiosity provides a mindset that bypasses the emotional baggage so often associated with choosing to care about the people who you don't yet know well.

Curiosity provides new perspectives that allow you to make better choices about the people who work in your organization, how they work with you individually and what influences them more effectively moving forward.

Diffusing Drama

At a previous company, I was at my desk one day when a manager came barreling out of her office and started to berate the young man sitting at the desk to my left. He was new, had been asked to complete a minor task, and it was not completed to her expectations. After her tirade, I visited her office. I was curious about what results she was expecting from this new employee. She and I had worked together for a while, and I knew she had a short temper, but I also knew that she had wanted to become better at communicating her expectations to others. She paused; her angry look started to change as she was thinking this through. Then she sighed as she realized that her angry reaction to such a small event was unnecessary, especially when it was direction at such a new employee who was still in training.

We talked about how she could have approached this. "Can you simply be curious first?" I asked. She looked puzzled. I suggested that she ask the new employee what information he was working with when he completed the assignment before she assumed anything. A while later, he was seen leaving her office, and she approached me. She had not given him the information she thought she had, there had been a miscommunication, and they discussed a new approach to communicating more effectively. She was grateful she had learned more about him, and was able to understand how to work together with more compassion. This is the silver lining of curiosity.

Gossip

Bert came into the lunch room area and sat down by me in a huff. He proceeded to outwardly gossip about how another coworker talked on the phone, ate at his desk and was generally a sloppy person, and he concluded that he was a slacker! Thankfully, no one else was in the lunch room to overhear this. Opinions spread quickly, and rumors grow teeth. I rested my sandwich on my plate, and asked him if he worked with that coworker often. He had. "What's his work like?" I asked. He then conceded that his work was pristine and completed on time. He confessed that he was bewildered by how someone with such clever work could appear so sloppy. The visual didn't meet the work output, and it confused him. "So, this is more about you than him?" I lightly chided. He begrudged, "You're right — it's about me, not him." We laughed a little, and I asked what would have happened if this got back to his coworker. The look on his face said it all. We discussed starting from a place of curiosity when starting a conversation with his coworker. He left with a plan of action that involved more compassion than judgement.

When curiosity is introduced, there is a positive shift to exploration. In this way, curiosity can diffuse the negative drama associated with gossip. Curiosity provides more openness and generosity to the other person. It may take repeated effort here, but curiosity provides the opportunity to shut down the need to gossip and offers the openness to see the other person with more compassion and humanity.

Emotions

Single parenting is hard. It is wrought with intense feelings to provide support for kids while being effective at work. A friend recently recounted her experience of getting back into the workforce after years as a stay-at-home mom. She had suffered a recent divorce and had custody of her kids and, one day, the need arose for her to leave work early due to an issue at her child's school. She was emotionally stressed at how she would be perceived at work while also trying to be an effective parent. She remembers fondly how her manager asked her a few questions and then easily gave her the grace to leave and take care of her child's needs without retribution or penalty. The emotional relief was profound.

He, too, had been a single parent and understood being compassionate with others, the same way he needed it himself. By using compassion, he was building a more compassionate and effective organization with employees who could tap into their humanity when making decisions.

When people become emotional, they may come to you and be angry, feel marginalized or express any range of emotions. Don't ignore their emotional state; address it with curiosity and care. When you use genuine and kind curiosity to explore what outcomes they desire, their emotions are then prompted to shift to venture into exploring the cause of their feelings, and discover what current ideas or new outcomes are more genuinely desired.

Mental exploration provides the space necessary to see situations from different perspectives. Collecting different perspectives drives compassion in actions and decision-making; solutions evolve quicker with curiosity.

Increasing Accountability

A team member on a project was becoming very difficult to work with. Deadlines were getting pushed back when her work wasn't provided to others. It was agreed that someone needed to discuss this with her, and I volunteered. I started the conversation with curiosity, asking her to help me identify hurdles in the project that made it difficult to meet deadlines — not just for her, but for others too. She easily blamed myriad extenuating circumstances, and seemed to assume that these were affecting others the same way. Explaining the lack of complaints by others, I confessed to being puzzled about how to move forward to meet the project deadline. She hesitated as she wrestled with an answer. I asked if we could get curious and discuss each hurdle she presented so we could figure out solutions. It was impressive how quickly she realized the insignificance of each hurdle. What evolved was identifying the need for tighter communication about individual deadlines on the team; and this resulted in her stepping up to provide a new idea on how to communicate more effectively as a team.

Often the person who seems to be the problem may be the exact person who identifies a solution. If I had tackled this as if the problem was just her, the whole team may have never gotten on a better page. The team would have suffered. This is how curiosity drives compassion. Curiosity sets emotions aside, invokes insight into cause and effect, and invites conversations that allow people to step up.

Driving Innovative Results

I recently heard Hal Gregersen, the executive director of the MIT Leadership Center, speak in Washington, D.C. His research focuses on what the most successful leaders do to keep themselves engaged and maintain long-term success. Interestingly, these leaders are terminally curious — they constantly seek out information in innovative ways.

Hal confirmed that one of the largest leadership pain points is the continual feed of positive data rather than the negative things that would drive better decisions. This is not done maliciously; people get into habits of bragging about what is going right first — it is the "don't fix what ain't broke" mindset. But, this habit doesn't make you a top leader. Hal found that to stay ahead of this scenario, the best leaders question everything, and find answers in innovative ways.

He relayed a story about an executive who chooses to have a company delivery driver pick him up when visiting his internationally located businesses instead of taking a limousine. This practice provides the opportunity to be curious and ask questions about the company from the eyes of those who are the working backbone of his company. These unique insights allow him to compassionately understand what his employees — outside the boardroom — need, what problems create hardships, and he gains their perspectives about workable solutions.

Indeed, even Jeff Bezos of Amazon fame regularly schedules time to work in almost every one of his company's positions to drive understanding, and to identify innovative and compassionate ways to improve as the company grows.

When leaders need to brainstorm innovative ideas, using curiosity becomes a vital tool to drive new ideas, fresh solutions and the ability to look at problems differently. This provides new space for conversations they would not have addressed if they only acted on assumptions or the readily-provided information.

Company-Wide Compassion

Booz Allen Hamilton continually polls their employees to understand and maximize best practices within their organization to create an inclusive culture; this provides a rich database. In August 2017, Hurricane Harvey dealt a blow to Texas in historic proportions. Booz Allen Hamilton knew they had employees either living in the area or who had family and friends affected by the event. Community service is among one of the organization's pivotal core values. To support this, immediately upon the onset of clean-up efforts, Booz Allen Hamilton sent out a company-wide email announcing that they would match any individual contributions, up to $50,000 *per* person, to donate funds to help those recovering from the effects of Harvey. This allowed employees who felt helpless and far away to make a greater impact than they could do on an individual scale. This represents putting their money where their values are, and is a compassionate gesture from the top down that supports the same compassion from its own employees.

The ability to be so readily compassionate came first from gathering information. Being curious about what was meaningful to each employee and what positively influenced their entire workforce was what drove Booz Allen Hamilton to strategically gather the information they needed to support the direction of the company's culture. This begs the question: How are you strategically curious?

Nurturing Richer Conversations

I sat in on a friend's project discussion recently. I was visiting and they hoped an outside perspective would provide new insights. The team was stuck on how to incorporate everyone's ideas. Knowing that we often overthink things, I simply started being curious. I asked questions as a novice. Having to explain to a "novice" offered them new insights into how their ideas would support each other's ideas.

Then I asked them to ask questions based upon their individual curiosity about each aspect, and each other's part, of the project. The brainstorming began, but the questions were new this time. They were genuinely interested in what each other had to offer from a place of curiosity. Several solutions were forming, laughter emerged and energy increased; this was a team indulging in richer brainstorming.

Curiosity offers nice gifts. Conversations emerge every day at work and in life. When we choose to be curious about someone, simply asking a question can start a unique conversation that provides novel insights and nurtures more daily interaction. New insights drive energy rather than subtract from it. More important, they provide richer details in one another's lives that support compassion in future decision-making.

Curiosity as a Vital Tool

When I started working out again, I was weak from chemotherapy. I could only use a 5-lb. dumbbell to exercise. With continued use, I increased weight but it was that 5-lb. dumbbell that got me started. Curiosity is like that 5-lb. weight — easy to lift in small doses, and with continued use, you get stronger. Using curiosity often will allow you to have richer conversations, diffuse unnecessary drama and be kind when emotions are high. Curiosity provides a useful context to explore accountability and innovation. Richer conversations will provide you with new insights and knowledge that will allow you to make more informed and compassionate decisions that affect those you work with and employ. This is a unique key to maximizing your leadership abilities and how you influence those around you.

What You Can Do NOW

Leadership is about taking care of, and positively influencing, other people. Alas, some leaders do not display habits that drive compassion down into their organizations. We, as individuals, can impact this significantly if we take responsibility within our own circles of influence. This is where the use of empathic curiosity can change every aspect of working with others.

Where do we start the process that leads to compassion? Ask a fellow employee, "What are you curious about?" Ask what outcomes to a problem they desire. Whatever the question, ask with openness and no agenda. Listen. Ask another question. Listen. Then take a moment and reflect. Notice how your thought process changes from the judgements you already might have had about that person to an open space, ready to learn.

This simple 5-lb. tool will provide you with a 100-lb. payoff in terms of results. The "small lifting" of asking about others can provide you with massive amounts of good will, interaction, innovative ideas and richer conversations. These conversations provide details about your people, and provide more accurate information about who, what and how company decisions impact employees. What's more, these conversations are inherently compassionate, and compassionate leadership generates remarkable results.

Get Curious!

About the Author

Carole Stizza, SHRM-SCP

Carole is CEO and Founder of Relevant Insight. A senior HR professional, Carole holds a Bachelor's and Master's in Industrial-Organizational Psychology, and has supported her military family in moves across the U.S. for 26 years until finally settling in Northern Virginia. During her relocations, Carole reached top leadership levels in sales organizations by crafting solid recruitment and customer service methods, consulted for the National Confectioners Association's Annual convention for more than 10 years in customer service and facilitation roles, and transitioned into HR roles to maximize her impact on organizational effectiveness.

Currently consulting, training and coaching, Carole speaks on current "pain points" that hold people and organizations back from true engagement. Addressing issues revolving around communicating your value, promoting accountability and unlocking relevant feedback, she has discovered that curiosity drives compassion faster than any other tool.

Carole's training and coaching techniques are steeped in her educational background, research and experiences. She has the ability to both ask the right questions and help clients arrive at the right answers for themselves; she speaks on how to utilize feedback, build interviewing skills and identify leadership blind spots to drive clarity in conversations. Through coaching and training, she helps individuals and companies optimize feedback and compassionate curiosity to expand employee engagement, and improve interview and performance success. Her clients range from college graduates and young professional millennials, to corporate executives, business owners and human resource departments across the country.

In her free time, Carole likes to travel, visit friends and work out. However, she is delighted to note that if she could laugh and dance to good music all day, she might stop going to the gym and still be very, very fit and happy.

Learn more and contact Carole:
carole@relevant-insight.com
LinkedIn.com/in/carolestizza
Twitter.com/relevant4you
Facebook.com/relevant4you

Chapter 15

♥

Shelly Trent

"Mental Health Issues in the Workplace: Cause for Compassion or Concern?"

If an employee showed up to work with a broken arm, you would make sure she got to a doctor. What about an employee who is suffering from depression and crying at his desk? Would you tell him to cheer up or ignore it? You might think that mental illness is something that only happens to "other people," but it is quite common in the workplace. In fact, even you may suffer from a mental health issue. If you answer "yes" to any of these questions, you probably do.

- Does the stress of your job make you so anxious that you need anti-stress medications to cope?
- Does your workplace productivity wane from depression and anxiety?
- Do you use substances such as alcohol, food or medication, to deal with the stress of work?
- Do you have trouble falling asleep or staying asleep because of worry?
- Do you get angry about minor issues, such as getting cut off in traffic, because you are stressed?

We applaud celebrities for talking about their mental health struggles, knowing that it may benefit others, and we look up to them for bravery in sharing their most personal secrets. For example, actress Gabourey Sidibe shared that she has battled depression and panic attacks; Elizabeth Vargas of ABC News announced that she suffers from anxiety and alcoholism; and musician Pete Wentz struggles with bipolar disorder. Dr. Harris Stratyner, Associate Clinical Professor of Psychiatry at the Sinai Medical Center, said, "When it comes to things like psychiatric illness and substance abuse, there's a stigma that's attached. When a celebrity who is respected comes out and reveals it, it's very empowering — particularly to young men and women — but to people of all ages."

♥   *So, if we admire celebrities for sharing their mental health issues, why do we condemn our employees?*

Dr. Anna Wachtel, a psychiatrist and founder of PsychiatryForHealth. com stated, "It's just like suffering from diabetes, high blood pressure or high cholesterol. What's the difference? There's absolutely zero difference. That's how we should view it."

The Reality of Mental Health Issues

We spend more time at work than we do with our loved ones. We are expected to be at the top of our game for at least eight hours a day, five (or more) days per week. We are supposed to keep our personal lives separate from work, so our private health issues don't interfere with our ability to be key producers for our organizations. Because we place value on success in our jobs, if we are not able to meet the demands, sometimes we get sick, depressed or anxious. For many, our sense of purpose and self-esteem is measured by how successful we are at work. Who we are at work is "who we are," sometimes.

Although we do not talk about it often, mental health is still considered a taboo topic. You may not be aware of the challenges that are

considered mental health issues. They include alcoholism, substance use/
abuse, ADHD, anxiety, depression, bipolar disorder, obsessive compul-
sive disorder, phobias, impulse-control, emotional trauma/PTSD,
autism, caregiving concerns, eating disorders, sleep disorders, postpartum
depression, workplace violence, anger management, suicidal tenden-
cies and more.

Workplace Mental Health Data

The Anxiety Disorders Association of America reports that 30 percent of
workers "have taken prescription medication to manage stress, nervous-
ness, emotional problems or lack of sleep and 28 percent have had an
anxiety or panic attack." Unmanaged personal stress can make us sick
— physically and mentally. We worry about telling our bosses out of fear
that we will be seen as a whiner, a complainer, unable to handle life or
requesting special treatment. We dread being labeled weak, unwilling or
unable to do the work, not getting promoted or having a negative report
in our personnel file. We don't want to risk our private business being
shared with others at work.

There is a stigma that comes with being labeled "mentally unstable." We
may consider using our organization's Employee Assistance Program
(EAP), but we worry that our employer will discover it and damage
our reputation. Instead, we visit our doctor and ask for medication to
help us cope.

Consider these facts from the Partnership for Workplace Mental Health:

- 70 percent of people with depression are in the workforce
- 26 percent of workers need mental health treatment
- Mental health treatment saves employers $2,000 per employee
- Most alcoholics work full-time.

Further, Officevibe.com compiled these startling statistics:

- Untreated mental health disorders have resulted in a $79 billion annual loss to companies from lower productivity and absenteeism.

- Depression results in more time off than heart disease, hypertension or diabetes.

- Mood disorders are estimated to cost more than $50 billion per year in lost productivity and more than 300 million days off for employees.

Here are three true stories of mental illness in the workplace that balance the hard facts noted above. In reviewing these case studies, do you think the employer dealt with them compassionately, fairly and legally? What were the business implications of each decision?

Stacy's Stress

Stacy had to take time off to care for her father who had been diagnosed with terminal cancer. Stacy kept up with her job as well as she could, working on projects while at the hospital sitting at her father's bedside until he passed. She had spent a month not only sitting with him at the hospital, but also checking on his house each day, bringing in the mail, paying his bills, feeding his pets and keeping the grass cut. In addition, Stacy had to talk with the hospital staff each day, work with hospice, make difficult decisions, gather all her father's "final wishes" paperwork and sell his home. As you can imagine, these were emotionally challenging tasks.

During this time, Stacy contacted her doctor about managing her stress, and he prescribed anti-anxiety medications and suggested a grief counselor. Unfortunately, Stacy had a reaction to the medications that made her angry, irritable and even suicidal. The doctor encouraged Stacy to stay on the medications until they had more time to work, but

her anxiety continued to worsen. After months of debilitating personal
and work-related stress, Stacy felt that her life was out of control. She
didn't want to lose her job, but she became overwhelmed to the point
of considering voluntary entry into a mental health center to cope with
what she felt was a nervous breakdown.

Stacy shared some of this with her supervisor, who was not kind given
the situation; he called Stacy multiple times to tell her it was time for her
to move on or that she'd be happier somewhere else. Stacy told him she
really wanted to keep her job, but he persisted in finding fault with everything Stacy did, likely to push her into leaving. Stacy went to human
resources to ask for an accommodation because she feared she was going
to be fired, and discovered that her boss had gone to HR soon afterward
to discuss her firing. Because she had asked for an accommodation, she
was not terminated at that time, but the relationship with her superiors
never healed. She was eventually let go due to her inability to handle the
constant unrealistic demands and stress purposefully placed on her by her
supervisor.

In this situation, Stacy might have pursued an accommodation where she
consistently worked with HR and her supervisor for a longer period of
time. Her supervisor, realizing that Stacy's personal stress was affecting
her work, could have been more understanding, accommodating Stacy
by lowering expectations for a time or allowing coworkers to assist Stacy
until her situation was resolved.

Michael's Malady

Michael developed panic anxiety disorder (PAD) after his time in the
military. PAD can strike at any time, such as during a sound sleep, so it
isn't necessarily triggered by an event or situation. He takes daily anxiety
medication to curb attacks.

Michael also takes a different prescribed medication for his PAD after an attack begins. The medicine is strong enough that Michael needs to "sleep it off" until the drug is out of his system. His employer understands that, occasionally, Michael may take a day or part of a day off until his medication wears off, and he is able to drive and function normally.

About once a year, the PAD is so severe that Michael is hospitalized. Michael's coworkers and supervisor are compassionate about his PAD and visit him in the hospital, so Michael doesn't worry that he will be let go.

Chris's Condition

Chris has severe insomnia. He has tried several different medications and over-the-counter supplements to help him sleep, but nothing seems to work. His doctors can do nothing more to help him. Normally, he falls asleep between 4:00 and 5:00 a.m.

He works from home, so he can put in work hours in the middle of the night when he can't sleep. Chris feels that as long as he completes his work and he puts in at least eight hours per day, there shouldn't be a problem. He is always on time for conference calls, even when they are early in the morning. He gets high marks on his performance reviews for good work and meeting deadlines.

However, his boss doesn't like that Chris is not always responsive to email early in the morning, because Chris has usually just fallen asleep. Chris explains to his boss that he has severe insomnia, but that he always finishes his work, even if his hours are odd. His boss isn't sympathetic about his sleep patterns and wants him to work from 8:00 a.m. to 5:00 p.m. like his coworkers. While he tries to do that, he finds himself falling asleep at his computer some afternoons due to lack of restful nighttime sleep. The cycle continues to worsen until Chris is let go for sleeping on the job.

In this case, the employer could have been innovative in accommodating his condition, which was well-documented. After all, Chris was productive and met his deadlines. His boss's expectations were just different from what he was physically able to satisfy, and ultimately, these expectations were not supportive of Chris or the company.

Showing Compassion

So, what can employers do to be more responsive and compassionate to mental health issues in the workplace? Start by encouraging your employees to share information about their mental health without fear of reprisal. If you help them with their challenges, they will be loyal and dedicated employees. In the summer of 2017, an Olark employee's email about taking a few "mental health days" went viral after her CEO responded that mental health days should be standard practice for all organizations to give employees time off without stigma. If your organization requires proof of illness to take sick time (e.g., many companies require that employees provide a doctor's note if they take more than two sick days in a row), you may want to make some time available without a doctor's note.

As an organization, be sure that leaders will not use an employee's admission of having a mental health issue as a reason to monitor their behavior or as a reason for termination. Ensure that supervisors will keep the information confidential, as some employees may not be supportive or could make the situation worse by ridiculing the individual.

By law, employers must respect privacy rights, unless there is cause to believe that the employee's condition could compromise safety. The Americans with Disabilities Act and the Equal Employment

Opportunity Act prohibit discrimination against people with disabilities in the workplace, and this includes psychiatric disabilities. Employers are required to offer reasonable accommodations if requested.

Offer mandatory training programs about mental health. Make it acceptable to talk openly about it. If anyone in leadership has a struggle to share, that will make others more apt to discuss their own challenges. Another author in this anthology, Jason Sackett (see Chapter 11), who is a Certified Employee Assistance Professional, said, "Destigmatizing mental health issues and encouraging help-seeking requires constant reinforcement, and if companies have an EAP (internal or external), that program should be messaging employees continuously on the benefits of mental health support and self-care."

If employees are suffering from substance abuse or have a disorder requiring in-patient treatment, allow them a period of time off without pay, but guarantee their job will be secure when they return.

Simple Ways to Show Compassion

Quick Wins:

- Allow employees to take walk breaks to get out of the office.
- Start lunch support groups for employees who struggle with similar conditions.
- Explain the value and privacy of your EAP.
- Offer relaxation, stress-management, anger-management and addiction-cessation classes.
- Create a healthy environment at work, as exercising in a group and eating healthier could lower employee stress levels.

- Invite a mental health provider to speak at your company so that employees can be educated about mental health symptoms and coping.

- Send flowers to someone who is dealing with a crisis.

- Prepare meals for employees who are going through a difficult time.

Policy Changes:

- Let employees adjust their work hours, schedule, tasks, and/or work setting sometimes.

- Create a sick bank where employees can donate their unused sick leave to someone in need.

- Involve employees in creating policies regarding mental health, and once the policy is drafted, have an attorney and a mental health professional review it.

CEOs Against Stigma, an organization that shares data about the impact of mental health in the workplace, reports, "CEOs who care about productivity will recognize they can't afford not to seek an end to stigma. Certainly, empathy for the suffering of fellow workers is, in itself, a strong motivator for most CEOs. But quite apart from empathy, the numbers make the case that ignoring stigma is bad for business." The organization also found that "employees who received high-quality depression care management over two years realized a 28 percent improvement in absenteeism and a 91 percent improvement in presenteeism," which led to "an estimated annual savings of $1,982 per full-time equivalent."

According to www.workplacementalhealth.org, "When employees receive effective treatment for mental illnesses, the result is lower total medical costs, increased productivity, lower absenteeism and decreased disability costs."

It isn't difficult for your organization to show compassion to employees with mental health challenges. Employers would be unwise to think workers with mental health issues don't have talents and value to offer. Some employees would forego higher salary to work in an organization where they and their illness would be accepted. As the data cited in this article show, mental health conditions cost organizations millions of dollars from lost productivity every year. When you address mental health in your workplace, you also address employee retention, loyalty and productivity.

In the field of human resources, we are told to be fair and consistent, and to treat everyone the same. When you are dealing with employees who have a mental illness, however, you need greater compassion and creativity with accommodations to support their needs and ultimately to benefit from their strengths and full potential. If an employee were blind or deaf, missing a limb or had cancer, you would accommodate their disability or illness. We need to approach mental illness with the same compassion as physical illness, and improve on accommodating mental health conditions at work.

About the Author

Shelly Trent, SPHR, SHRM-SCP, CAE

Shelly Trent is a career coach, writer, speaker and educator in Human Resources. She has more than 16 years' experience working for the Society for Human Resource Management (SHRM). Aside from human resources, Shelly's background includes university continuing education, college career

services and business and industry training; she is a specialist in adult career development.

She serves as an adjunct faculty member at Indiana University Southeast's School of Business, where she teaches business students about career planning and job search skills. She also was assistant editor of and writer for the National Career Development Association's Career Convergence magazine for three years, and has written and contributed to numerous other published works in the area of career development.

Shelly has completed her PhD coursework (all but dissertation) in HRD/OD and career counseling at the University of Louisville. In addition, she holds a Master of Public Administration and a BA in Government, Writing and Criminology from Western Kentucky University.

Shelly is married, and has two cats and one dog — all rescues. In her free time, she enjoys weather (she's a certified storm spotter), cookie baking, family genealogy and collecting Beatles' memorabilia. Her Myers-Briggs type is INFJ.

Learn more and contact Shelly:
Shellytrent@live.com
Twitter.com/HRDShelly
LinkedIn.com/in/shellytrent

Chapter 16

♥

Laura Hillerich Wood

"When the Wind Blows, Hope Grows"

Can you imagine a day when your life changes so drastically that it seems nothing will ever be the same again? In 2005, I was working for Kindred Healthcare and our employees in New Orleans had that horrible experience. As a result, I had the chance to be involved in and see firsthand the evolution of true compassion at work; I experienced a company's ability to engage the "Human Spirit" in the darkest of times.

My co-workers and I were slated to make a trip to New Orleans to conduct Human Resource training for the Chief Clinical Officers of our Long Term Acute Care Hospitals (LTAC). The trip was planned during hurricane season the week of August 29, 2005; of particular interest to all who would be traveling was the tropical depression forming over the Bahamas. Having never traveled to New Orleans, I asked others about the likelihood of our trip needing to be postponed. The consensus was that it had been more than 36 years since a hurricane had hit New Orleans; we would move ahead as planned.

On the morning of August 29, heavy rain had been falling for hours, but no one could have known exactly what was yet to come. That morning, by the time Hurricane Katrina (a Category 3 storm) struck New Orleans, a storm surge as high as 29 ½ ft. in some places, arrived; it overwhelmed many of the city's levees and brought sustained winds of up to 140 miles per hour.

The storm itself did a great deal of damage, but its aftermath was catastrophic. Many people felt that the government was slow to respond in providing assistance to the people affected by the storm. Predominantly, the federal government seemed unprepared for the disaster. The Federal Emergency Management Agency (FEMA) took days to set up recovery operations in New Orleans and, even then, they didn't have a solid action plan. For example, when my company procured buses to transport our employees and patients to safety, FEMA took those vehicles not just from us, but many other employers trying to evacuate their staff, and left those vehicles unused in a parking lot for more than a week.

Our trip had been canceled, so from our corporate office in Louisville, Kentucky, we watched and listened in horror. Once it was determined that our hospital — having been built at a higher elevation — was dry and the backup generators were working, a game plan started to come together. We were relying mainly on TV news to learn what was happening and didn't understand why TV crews were there and the National Guard wasn't. From what we were seeing, we had good reason to be concerned about the safety of our hospital staff and patients, as mass looting was occurring; any standing business that distributed pharmaceuticals was at great risk.

Our CEO and Hospital Division President, with the assistance of the leadership teams, were fast at work to find out as much as they could about the status of our employees and the patients. This posed tremendous challenges because the phone lines were down in some places; many places had no electricity; and subsequently, cell phone batteries were dying. The initial desire was to charter a private plane to have someone there that could assess the status of our facility, but all airline travel was suspended.

At that time, we had more than 290 employees working at the New Orleans hospital. Of course, they were not all working that morning but, due to the timing of the disaster, the employees who had been there overnight — along with limited relief staff who reported for their morning shifts — were unable to leave until the entire facility could be evacuated. Beyond that, we had no way of knowing where people were. Ray Nagin, the mayor of New Orleans, didn't issue the mandatory evacuation of the city until Saturday night, August 27, a week later than other cities and counties along the Gulf Coast; therefore, we had no idea which of our staff and their families had evacuated.

One of our first plans of action was a letter from the President and CEO of the company to the Kindred employees of our New Orleans hospital and their families. This letter was posted on major media publications and websites such as *USA Today*, both print and online. The letter advised individuals who were impacted by Katrina to call an employee assistance toll-free line so we could ensure that they were safe and to make them aware of available resources. This hotline was available 24 hours a day, seven days a week.

Many team members at our corporate office, across divisions, expressed the desire to help. They signed up for shifts to handle the phones. I will never forget the calls I answered in the ensuing weeks, as people in the hurricane-affected region expressed desperation like I had never heard before. Calls from family members who had evacuated the city and were desperate to know the status of their loved ones who were still at the hospital. Calls from employees who had no access to money because their banks were flooded. Calls of appreciation for the hope we were giving to those living through one of the worst natural disasters of their lives. Hope — although intangible — was needed by all and was absolutely priceless.

Beyond the employee assistance line, other services were provided to employees, including the following:

- An allocation of money was available for employees impacted, and they could call the assistance line twice to request funds. Once they identified where they were physically located, money was wired to a Wells Fargo location close to them. Although it wasn't a large amount of money, it would be enough for them to purchase necessities for themselves and their families.

- We paid all staff, full and part-time, for two weeks' work.

- Because the situation in New Orleans was dire and reopening of the hospital was uncertain, employees could review all openings in our system anywhere in the United States (and not just with LTAC hospitals), and apply for a transfer without having to complete the normal transfer and placement process.

- Employees were also able to utilize the Employee Assistance Program (EAP), which was available for emotional, psychological and other support. All services are free for employees, confidential and accessible 24 hours a day. The EAP provided immediate help during this crisis when emotional needs could reach a critical point.

The response from employees was one of extraordinary generosity; out of this generosity, the HOPE (Helping Others Persevere through Emergencies) Fund — a 501(c)(3) charitable organization — was created. I was very blessed and fortunate to be on the first HOPE fund committee, and was thankful to be part of the team that crafted the program. Our communicated mission was and still is to provide monetary assistance to employees experiencing financial hardship due to catastrophic life events such as:

- Death

- Natural disaster

- Medical hardship

- Homelessness or

- Other catastrophic life events.

The process for employees to request assistance due to a financial crisis brought on by a catastrophic event simply involves contacting their facility leader or supervisor; if the situation is such that the employee is unable to make the call themselves, their direct supervisor can initiate it on their behalf.

Since the beginning of the program, there have been many examples of the way employees have been helped beyond the first recipients who suffered significant loss from Hurricane Katrina. There have been employees who have lost homes or had significant damage due to tornadoes, families involved in terrible car accidents, an employee diagnosed with a terminal illness and the list goes on. Letters of gratitude have been received that are poignant. Time and time again it has been said how fortunate the recipients are to work with such generous and thoughtful people. Not only is this what compassion at work looks like, but also a definite representation of a workplace that engages the human spirit.

Today, The HOPE Fund doesn't just exist — it thrives, thanks to the conscious decision of employees to help each other through regular contributions. Since 2005, 4,550 employees have received assistance through the fund, and $5,325,670 has been distributed.

Although I am no longer employed at Kindred Healthcare, I still have great memories and admiration for their continued commitment to offer compassion at work. I have recently observed that, although it has been more than 12 years since the devastation of Katrina, the HOPE Fund is once again being used to help employees who were affected by more recent natural disasters, such as Hurricanes Harvey, Irma and Marie. In addition, I've learned of other employers who have similar employee funds and are actively engaged in assisting employees in their time of need.

Compassion at work and the creation of workplaces that engage the human spirt are possible and more than just lip service or a plaque on the wall covered in dust that recognizes a company's mission and values. Companies must believe it, heart and soul. It is not only possible but necessary now more than ever. Human beings are more than just their jobs; they are living, breathing creations of God. As such, we can contribute in great ways to a business's success. But, employees need to feel that the company is invested in them not just as an employee, but as the whole person — the one who is faced with a life-changing event, both good and bad. How can we do more to provide compassion for our employees during or after the birth or adoption of baby? In the wake of an unexpected death? After a medical diagnosis for themselves or a family member? After a natural disaster that changes their lives forever?

As an HR professional who has worked with employers across industries, I have seen that, due to business necessity and the bottom line, companies can lose sight of the individuals who are the key component to business success. More times than I can say, I have been in conversations where "compassion at work" is considered "warm and fuzzy," and not always seen as something that can result in tangible, real-time business results. Compassion — now, more than ever — is needed in the workplace. I know this from personal experience, and believe it is supported by a recent Gallup workplace survey that found that 26 percent of the workforce is disengaged, 45 percent are partially engaged and just 29 percent are fully engaged. I trust this is the reality of modern-day employee engagement, and that, although these results are unsettling, they can be resolved.

♥   *Even in the face of the unthinkable, organizations can be their very best.*

When the wind blows, hope can grow, as it did for my Kindred colleagues in the wake of Hurricane Katrina. I encourage businesses that are seeking to either continue or expand their compassion at work programs — and those that are interested in implementing one — to give it serious thought. It is possible for employers to make compassion at work part of their mission and values, and for it to have far-reaching positive benefits for people and profits. I have lived "compassion at work" first hand, and assure you that it is not only possible, but achievable and sustainable.

"Compassion is an irreplaceable dimension of excellence for any organization that wants to make the most of its human capabilities."
— Monica Worline and Jane Dutton —

About the Author

Laura Hillerich Wood, SHRM-CP, PHR

Laura Hillerich Wood is a collaborative HR business partner. She has more than 20 years' experience as a human resources leader, with experience in: healthcare, including hospitals, senior living and nursing homes; financial services/banking; and distribution/shipping/ supply chain management and has worked with both profit and non-profit organizations. Her established reputation is for creating partnerships with individuals at all levels — both internally and externally — including C-suite leaders.

Laura's proficiency and passion cover many areas, from talent acquisition to onboarding and retention, and the use of staff recognition; staff training and development; supervision; employee relations; mediation; advocacy; and conflict resolution techniques. Her expertise in understanding the overall intricacies of HR in multiple industries also allows her to interpret and counsel on issues pertaining to the implications of employment law.

Laura holds a BS in Business from Mid-Continent University.

Aside from human resources, Laura's passion is her family, friends and her church. She and her husband have five adult children and seven grandchildren. In her free time, she enjoys spending time with her husband, including spending time on the lake or river sailing, kayaking or rowing; cheering on their favorite sports teams, University of Louisville Cards (hers), Virginia Tech Hokies (his) — always a friendly rivalry. In addition, Laura loves singing with her church choir, reading and traveling when she can get away.

Learn more and contact Laura:
Lawood0331@gmail.com
Twitter.com/LWoodHRpro
LinkedIn.com/in/laura-hillerich-wood
Facebook.com/HillerichWood

100% of the Publisher Proceeds from the Amazon Sales of this Book Will Benefit the SHRM Foundation

The SHRM Foundation is a values-based charity organization whose mission is to champion workforce and workplace transformation by providing research-based HR solutions for challenging inclusion issues facing current and potential employees, scholarships to educate and develop HR professionals to make change happen and opportunities for HR professionals to make a difference in their local communities. The SHRM Foundation is a 501(c)(3) nonprofit organizational affiliate of the Society for Human Resource Management.

Learn more at www.shrm.org/foundation.

You@Work: Unlocking Human Potential in the Workplace

The next book in the @Work Series, due out Summer 2018.

If you are an HR or OD expert with interest in being a contributing author for a future @Work anthology, please contact Cathy Fyock at 502-445-6539 or Cathy@CathyFyock.com.